TORAH TO THE GENTILES
St. Paul's Letter to the Galatians

TORAH TO THE GENTILES
St. Paul's Letter to the Galatians

Marc Philip Boulos

OCABS PRESS
ST PAUL, MINNESOTA 55124
2014

TORAH TO THE GENTILES
St. Paul's Letter to the Galatians

Copyright © 2014 by
Marc Philip Boulos

ISBN 1-60191-031-2

PRINTED IN THE UNITED STATES OF AMERICA

Torah to the Gentiles
St. Paul's Letter to the Galatians

ISBN 1-60191-031-2

Published by OCABS Press, St. Paul, Minnesota.
Printed in the United States of America.

Books are available through OCABS Press at special
discounts for bulk purchases in the United States by
academic institutions, churches, and other organizations.
For more information please email OCABS Press at
press@ocabs.org.

The full text of Galatians is taken from the *Revised
Standard Version* and the *New Testament of the Greek
Orthodox Church.* All other scripture quotations are taken
from the *New American Standard Bible.* Where helpful,
transliteration of the Greek is included.

Cover art by Olga Ivkin.

To Alla

Foreword

There is a renewal underway in Orthodox biblical scholarship, most notably in the Antiochian School of exegesis as it has been revived in the writings of Paul Nadim Tarazi. The latter's emphasis on the hegemony of the Bible and commitment to grappling with the biblical text on its own terms has inspired a generation of clergy to search the gospel relentlessly, until "the pages of our bibles have been dirtied and torn from our handling."[1] This book is a product of Tarazi's school and owes no small debt to his teaching. On the occasion of his retirement, it is an attempt to repeat something old in a new way, offered in gratitude to God for "every good gift and every perfect gift" that is from above, always given as the fruit of other men's labor (James 1:17).

—Marc Boulos
September 14, 2014

---

[1] Paul Nadim Tarazi, "The Antiochian School of Biblical Exegesis." *Word Magazine*, January 1986, 7.

Table of Contents

Biblical Pedagogy

"The difference between the almost right word and the right word is really a large matter—it's the difference between the lightning bug and the lightning."

—Mark Twain[2]

I remember the first time I heard the gospel. I don't remember the sermon that followed. I remember the reading. I was just 10 years old. It was the Sunday before Nativity, the first Christmas after my mom's parents had passed away. Holding my candle attentively, I stood before the priest, straining to hear the long list of Hebrew names as he stumbled through Matthew's genealogy (Matthew 1:1–25). I had embraced my dad's understanding of Near Eastern patriarchy and lineage. It was never explained to me. I just picked it up from my dad. So I was puzzled—even shocked—by the genealogy's ending. "How," I thought, "could they call Jesus the son of David?" It was Joseph who was David's son, and he was not the father of Jesus. Even if Mary were a daughter of the same family, "Mary," I puzzled, *"cannot carry the line."* I had stumbled upon the right question—*Matthew's question.* Posed to a child without adult intervention and weathered by time and study, this nagging point continues to drive my "asking" and "knocking" on scripture's door,

[2] Hugh Rawson and Margaret Miner, *The Oxford Dictionary of American Quotations* (New York: Oxford University Press, 2006). Letter to George Bainton, October 5, 1888, reprinted as *Reply to the Editor of "The Art of Authorship,"* 1890.

as I "seek" the wisdom in its pages (Matthew 7:7). This personal experience embodies the mission and purpose of biblical pedagogy, which is to transform the human mind through the Bible's counter-logic, scandal, symbolic dissonance and non-conformity (Romans 12:2). It also explains why, as an adult, I am happy to read difficult literature to my children, irrespective of my opinion or their response.

On the whole, modern education does not hold the same respect for knowledge or a child's ability to learn. The NewSouth edition of Huckleberry Finn, which edits out controversial language such as "injun" and "nigger," is but one example. The latter was published in response to a growing consensus among American educators that Twain's edition is unsuitable for schoolchildren. The same attitude is found among American pastors, who cringe at biblical examples of violent judgment—applicable to their own communities—or blush when St. Paul refers to the sum total of his religious achievements as "shit" (σκύβαλον; Philippians 3:8). Thanks be to God, Paul was a scriptural teacher, not a modern "educator." C.S. Lewis famously anticipated the woes of modern education in his work, *The Abolition of Man:*

> *The difference between the old and the new education will be an important one. Where the old initiated, the new merely 'conditions.' The old dealt with its pupils as grown birds deal with young birds when they teach them to fly; the new deals with them more as the poultry-keeper deals with young birds—making them thus or thus for purposes of which the*

birds know nothing. In a word, the old was a kind of propagation—men transmitting manhood to men; the new is merely propaganda.[3]

Modern educators speak of learning how to think as though a child can learn to swim without jumping into water. Instead of doing the difficult work of teaching—which requires endless hours in the pool—we obsess over teaching methods and theories of education. We write classroom curricula as though what we say *about* Twain is more important than *Twain himself.* That might be true if the class were about the teacher, but for those who want to know exactly what Twain wrote and why, it is a scandal. In the end, our comfortable version of Twain is presented in lieu of empirical data. We do not deny that our siblings were once called "niggers," we just don't talk about it. We may acknowledge the existence of hatred, but in our curricula, we do not identify with it. We set ourselves above the painful reality of the world outside our imagination, because synthesis is safe and facilitates control. Worse, we stand ready to attack empirical data when it does not conform to our mental constructs. "To my amazement," wrote Dostoyevsky, "the more I love humanity in general, the less I love man in particular."[4] Dostoyevsky's pious rich woman epitomizes hypocrisy:

---

[3] C. S. Lewis, *The Abolition of Man* (New York: Harper Collins, 2009), 23.
[4] Fyodor Dostoyevsky, *The Brothers Karamazov* (New York: The Macmillan Company, 1922), 54.

the human tendency to whitewash ugliness with idealism.[5] In the case of the word "nigger," we sought to protect our mental empire by censoring America's most ardent proponent of abolition and emancipation.[6] Eventually, as our censorship unfolds, we find ourselves at war with creation itself, because its complexity and empirical diversity contradict the delusion that we are its masters.[7]

Despite the most noble intentions of modern education's imposed delusions, no amount of magical thinking can erase the displacement of Native Americans or the brutal subjugation of African slaves. Yet we proceed with censorship, in the hope that sheltering children from our own brutality will lead to a better world. This hypocritical delusion ignores a basic fact of the human condition: that we all share the same DNA and are prone to the same behaviors.

---

[5] Ibid. Madame Khokhlakov explains that her love for humanity calls her to charitable service, even as she complains of potentially abusive, rude or ungrateful beneficiaries.

[6] Philip S. Foner, *Mark Twain: Social Critic* (New York: International Publishers, 1958), 200.

[7] Nassim Nicholas Taleb, *The Black Swan: The Impact of the Highly Improbable* (New York: Random House Digital, Inc., 2007), xxx. In the field of economics, Nassim Taleb describes our proclivity for idealism as "platonicity," which, in the absence of empirical data, "makes us think that we understand more than we actually do."

In contrast with modern education, which idealizes humanity, the Bible[8] illustrates human behaviors and their outcomes, exposing our pervasive hypocrisy. Those who prefer the comfort of delusion complain that the Older Testament [9] is too violent, too negative, or too misogynistic. In reality, the numerous abuses recorded in the Bible are nothing more than a looking glass for the human race. In 2 Samuel, the prophet Nathan shoves this mirror in the king's face, forcing David to see himself in his condemnation of others. Hearing the prophet's report, David quickly condemns a rich man for stealing a poor man's lamb, unwittingly accusing himself:

> *Then David's anger burned greatly against the man, and he said to Nathan, 'As the Lord lives, surely the man who has done this deserves to die. He must make restitution for the lamb fourfold, because he did this thing and had no compassion.' Nathan then said to David: 'You are the man!'* (2 Samuel 12:1–7)

It was David, wealthy and powerful, who had murdered his subordinate, Uriah the Hittite, in order to steal his wife:

---

[8] Through my own study, I have come to see a unity of purpose in the myriad of sacred texts that form the canonical Bible. To detail this view here would be impractical. For the purposes of this book, I am assuming the continuity of the Bible's storyline.

[9] I prefer "Older Testament" to the more familiar, "Old Testament," since the latter wrongly implies expiration and/or separation from the New Testament.

> *Why have you despised the word of the Lord by doing evil in*
> *his sight? You have struck down Uriah the Hittite with the*
> *sword, have taken his wife to be your wife, and have killed*
> *him with the sword of the sons of Ammon. Now therefore, the*
> *sword shall never depart from your house, because you have*
> *despised me and have taken the wife of Uriah the Hittite to*
> *be your wife.' Thus says the Lord, 'Behold, I will raise up evil*
> *against you from your own household; I will even take your*
> *wives before your eyes and give them to your companion, and*
> *he will lie with your wives in broad daylight. Indeed you did*
> *it secretly, but I will do this thing before all Israel, and under*
> *the sun.' (2 Samuel 12:9–12)*

Nathan's simple honesty smashed David's idealized self-image. Zealously condemning the rich man in the parable, David was blind to his own role in victimizing his subordinate.

Likewise, in Matthew, Jesus exposes the Pharisees' religious piety as nothing but whitewash over their impurity:

> *Woe to you, scribes and Pharisees, hypocrites! For you are like*
> *whitewashed tombs which on the outside appear beautiful,*
> *but inside they are full of dead men's bones and all*
> *uncleanness. So you, too, outwardly appear righteous to men,*
> *but inwardly you are full of hypocrisy and lawlessness.*
> *(Matthew 23:27–28)*

The Pharisees *presume* the possibility of a pure or "good" person because they believe themselves—on the basis of appearance—better than those whose sins are outwardly visible. A well-dressed, tactful, middle class office worker who is privately arrogant is much harder to single out than a prostitute or a homeless drug addict. The latter is associated with uncleanness; the former with the eternal bliss of Middle America. In the Sermon on the Mount, Jesus is explicit: a godly man who obeys in secret is outwardly indistinguishable from the godless. [10] True purity, Jesus teaches, *is not visible.* The human being who sees purity is blind, because human eyes fool us into thinking that we can differentiate between pure and impure. In reality, human eyes are incapable of distinguishing a cruel act motivated by love from a kind act borne out of cruelty. That is why children *must* hear the Bible unfiltered: it is only the teaching—in whatever form it takes—not the teacher, that can penetrate their consciences.

In opposition to human idealism, the Bible asserts that there is *no such thing* as a good person (Psalm 14:1–3). In contrast with Dostoyevsky's pious rich woman, scripture is merciless in its honest portrayal both of individuals and of people in general. Perpetuating the David-Nathan paradigm, it repeatedly coaxes the ego, inviting condemnation of the sinner in order to expose its readers to their own hypocrisy:

> *Therefore you have no excuse, O man, whoever you are, when you judge another; for in passing judgment upon him you*

---

[10] Richard Benton, personal communication, December 23, 2013. See Matthew 6.

> *condemn yourself, because you, the judge, are doing the very*
> *same things. (Romans 2:1)*

By ruthlessly illustrating our behaviors, the scriptural God is in constant conflict with human beings. Paul's use of the expression, "whoever you are" is damning, since it applies the Lord's anger not just to Israel, but to *anyone* who hears his letter.

We pretend that our society has improved since the days of Twain because we whitewash his writing with the purified language of social piety.[11] In reality, we need look no further than the reservations and inner cities of today to see that we have not come to terms with the "niggers" and "injuns" of Twain's narrative. Like David, we judge the unjust while remaining blind to our own role in the perpetuation of injustice. Where our sanitized curricula fails miserably, the Bible succeeds, helping us see the truth about our behavior.

Teaching, not Obscuring

In illustrating the painful truth of our conduct, the Bible employs the most practical pedagogy of all, one that American educators would do well to reconsider. The teaching of God is handed down in the Bible as a collection of practical examples and illustrations, or *parables*.

---

[11] "Whitewash," see Ezekiel 13:10–14.

I will never forget my daughter's first experience of science class. Her teacher, open to the use of narrative, began her astronomy lesson by telling the story of Pegasus. That evening, my daughter spoke passionately about Pegasus and the beheading of Medusa, all the while integrating these metaphors with the monotonous star charts and constellations that were the subject of her class. Where Twain's censors obscure the actual source material, the narrative example of Pegasus helped a six-year-old girl integrate a complex set of data into her understanding of the world.

The biblical tradition, like astronomy, is a field of science. Whereas the modern sciences deal with the mechanics of the physical world, the Bible deals with types of human behavior and their predictable outcomes, or *fruit*. More than simply helping us understand this data, the Bible's stories document the causes and effects of our behaviors, and then demand specific actions based on the evidence provided. This mechanism in scripture is commonly referred to as *commandment* and *judgment*. If I slap someone on the face, I have no right to be offended when that person strikes back. Moreover, if I am the Bible's adherent, I must assume that it is *God himself* who is striking me. "Fracture for fracture," says the Lord, "eye for eye, tooth for tooth; whatever injury [man] has given a person shall be given to him" (Leviticus 24:20).

Such a practical approach in the form of narrative would have been appealing to the Romans, whose once sensible culture had been torn asunder by Hellenistic philosophy.[12] With the rise of Hellenism, individualism replaced duty to family, community, and state; emperor superseded constitution; and superstition overruled practical wisdom, leading to a general "deterioration in both social and political standards."[13] Not so on the Roman battlefield, where pragmatic wisdom remained a matter of life and death. As the Centurion explained, the practical dynamics of commandment and judgment were well known to him:

> *For I also am a man under authority, with soldiers under me; and I say to this one, 'Go!' and he goes, and to another, 'Come!' and he comes, and to my slave, 'Do this!' and he does it. (Matthew 8:9)*

The Centurion's ability to give correct instruction depends on his knowledge of the battlefield and his ability to anticipate the behavior of others. If his directives reflect reality on the ground, his men will be saved and the battle won. Should his instruction fail, the judgment against both him and his men is death. It is no wonder that Jesus explicitly approved of the Centurion's attitude (Matthew 8:10)! Insofar as the Bible's behavioral wisdom is based on repeatable, observable evidence, Hellenized Rome's resistance to the biblical movement stood little chance, no matter how fierce the persecutions.

---

[12] Cyril E. Robinson, "Hellenism and its Fruits, Section IV: Individualism," in *A History of the Roman Republic* (London: Thomas Y. Crowell Company Publishers, 1932), 230–232.
[13] Ibid.

There is another reason behind the Bible's teaching success. Unlike the lofty rhetoric of Hellenistic philosophy (1 Corinthians 2:1; Colossians 2:8), the stories of the Bible were written for the masses, to be easily understood by the average person. Like the story of Pegasus, the New Testament made it possible for the gentiles to integrate the Torah (the Hebrew word for *law, instruction,* or *teaching*) into their understanding of the world, despite complications arising from its foreign language and culture.

In the New Testament, God's Torah—*the Pentateuch*—is recapitulated in Paul's gospel, of which Jesus is the content and with which the Holy Spirit is "co-extensive and equivalent." [14] In fulfillment of the *Nevi'im* (the Prophets) and the *Ketuvim* (the Writings), in the story of the Bible, it is Jesus Christ, the Messiah, who carries the Torah to the Roman Empire, and beyond.

Today, the Bible is as foreign to our culture as it was to Roman society. Yet, instead of seeking to understand it on *its* terms, we arrogantly misjudge cultural references, stumble carelessly over poorly translated words, and misread ancient metaphor under an assumed modern context. Worse, we see contradiction where none exists and impose synthesis where contradiction is intended. Instead of dealing with the story's purposeful tensions, we preach a biblical curricula—our various theologies—in

---

[14] Paul Nadim Tarazi, *The New Testament: Luke and Acts* (Crestwood, New York: St. Vladimir's Seminary Press, 2001), 20.

which we hypocritically force the "no" of the Bible and the "yes" of the human being to coexist. Story after story, the scriptural God is ruthless in his naked depiction of human behavior. Despite this fact, American pastors ramble endlessly about a loving, gentle god who exists to coddle our insecurities and feed our narcissism. To which god are they referring? Certainly not, for example, the God of Isaiah:

> *See, the day of the Lord is coming—a cruel day, with wrath and fierce anger—to make the land desolate and destroy the sinners within it. The stars of heaven and their constellations will not show their light. The rising sun will be darkened and the moon will not give its light. I will punish the world for its evil, the wicked for their sins. I will put an end to the arrogance of the haughty and will humble the pride of the ruthless. I will make people scarcer than pure gold, more rare than the gold of Ophir. Therefore I will make the heavens tremble; and the earth will shake from its place at the wrath of the Lord Almighty, in the day of his burning anger. (Isaiah 13:9–13)*

Since Isaiah's Lord is altogether incompatible with the *loving-placebo-god* of our theologies, we filter Isaiah. We explain to our parishioners that what really counts is what our homiletic curricula says *about* Isaiah. We fashion a new god with our own hands, one that allows the most violent nation on earth to see itself as the good guy. Yet, Jesus reminds us, "No one is good but God alone" (Mark 10:18).

The Rejection of Temple Piety

Like an authoritarian parent, the Bible overcomes our persistent self-delusion with the constant and forceful repetition of behavioral instruction:

Love your enemies, do good to those who hate you, bless those who curse you, pray for those who mistreat you. (Luke 6:27–28)

Through paternalistic correction, judgment, and reiteration, the most difficult changes in behavior become intuitive, even *impulsive,* once the teaching penetrates the conscience. In that day, "declares the Lord, 'I will put my Torah within them and on their heart I will write it'" (Jeremiah 31:33; translation mine).

When our natural impulse is to love the neighbor according to God's Torah, we no longer seek any course of action that does not have the love of neighbor as its single priority. In the Older Testament, God struggles to teach this love by repeatedly making war with Jerusalem and eventually destroying its chief idol, the temple (Jeremiah 52, 2 Kings 25). The temple was perpetuating an ancient lie, that through correct piety, human beings could manipulate God's affections. Whereas the scriptural God offers the gift of life freely in Genesis, human beings seek a reciprocal relationship with him, in which love is replaced by a business transaction. Instead of trusting in God's generous promise, we attempt to purchase security from him with bribes. "Behold," the Lord assured Jacob,

"I am with you and will keep you wherever you go" (Genesis 28:15), to which the patriarch replied:

> *If God will be with me and will keep me on this journey that I take, and will give me food to eat and garments to wear, and I return to my father's house in safety, then the Lord will be my God. (Genesis 28:20–21)*

In his reply, Jacob assumes that the clay is able to bargain with the potter: *If* God does what I want, *then* I will serve him." "On the contrary," proclaims Paul, "who are you, O man, who answers back to God" (Romans 9:20)? In no small coincidence, before giving his answer, Jacob marveled at the place where he stood, calling it "none other than the house of God" (Genesis 28:17). Jacob's excitement at the prospect of building a new religious center is paralleled only by God's rejection of the temple in the Prophets:

> *Thus says the Lord: "Heaven is my throne and the earth is my footstool; what is the house which you would build for me, and what is the place of my rest? (Isaiah 66:1)*

Likewise, in Mark, when one of the disciples marveled at the temple complex and its surrounding buildings, Jesus replied, "Not one stone will be left upon another which will not be torn down" (Mark 13:2).

In the Older Testament, the temple's destruction demonstrates the folly of Israel's delusion, namely, that God can be controlled by human hands. John underlines this point by contrasting the temple made of stone with God's temple, Jesus Christ:

> *Jesus answered them, 'Destroy this temple, and in three days I will raise it up.' The Jews then said, 'It took forty-six years to build this temple, and will you raise it up in three days?' But he was speaking of the temple of his body. (John 2:19–21)*

By investing capital and manpower in a temple made of stone, the Jews opted for the false security of the work of their own hands, incompatible with the Lord's temple: a living person who is able to *hear* the Torah and to *walk* by the Spirit of its instruction. As a living, *speaking temple,* Jesus stands in contrast to idols made of stone:

> *Their idols are silver and gold, the work of man's hands. They have mouths, but they cannot speak; They have eyes, but they cannot see; They have ears, but they cannot hear; They have noses, but they cannot smell; They have hands, but they cannot feel; They have feet, but they cannot walk; They cannot make a sound with their throat. Those who make them will become like them, everyone who trusts in them. (Psalm 115:4–8)*

"The light" of God's Torah that fills his temple "shined in the darkness, but the darkness did not comprehend it" (John 1:5). Whereas the Lord had spared Isaac (Genesis 22:12), in their rejection of God's instruction, the people showed no mercy to Jesus (John 19:15). In the last salvo of an ancient and un-winnable war with God, by attacking Jesus, Israel and Rome had raised their hands in unison against the temple of God's heavenly city, the Jerusalem above (Galatians 4:26). Thankfully, God did not abandon his son to the brutality of human judgment, which condemns everything in its path to the futility of the grave.

Throughout the Older Testament, Jerusalem's destruction is a recurring marker, always coupled with its alternative: the *possibility* of life through Israel's trust in the Torah.

In his letter to the Galatians, Paul repeatedly makes this point by describing the confrontation between flesh (of human beings) and spirit (of God's instruction), pitting the teaching of men against the word of God; the latter being the only hope of life and resurrection.

Propagation, not Propaganda

Like David, each of us trusts in our ability to discern right from wrong. Building a false image of ourselves, we move on to build ideologies that impose our moral propaganda on the world around us. The book publisher builds a system of censorship; the educator, her curricula; the priest, his theology. Inevitably, the simplicity of these ideologies enables us to easily judge right from wrong and pure from impure at the expense of those whom we deem wrong or impure. Worse, in applying our judgments, we reinforce a misplaced trust in ourselves, establishing a cruel and inescapable cycle of self-righteousness. It is for such teachers—who distort or suppress the Bible's difficult message (Micah 2:6; Hosea 4:11)—that the Lord prepares his judgments, "visiting the iniquity of the fathers on the children" (Exodus 20:5):

> *My people are destroyed for lack of knowledge. Because you have rejected knowledge, I also will reject you from being my priest. Since you have forgotten the law of your God, I also will forget your children. The more they multiplied, the more they sinned against me; I will change their glory into shame. They feed on the sin of my people and direct their desire toward their iniquity; And it will be like people like priest; So I will punish them for their ways and repay them for their deeds. They will eat but not have enough; They will play the harlot but not increase, because they have stopped giving heed to the Lord. (Hosea 4:6–10)*

In Hosea, the priests "feed on the sin" of the people, sustaining themselves by refusing to preach the Torah. By emphasizing ritual and relaxing the Lord's instruction concerning conduct, they increase their wealth at the expense of the people's wellbeing.[15] Against such teachers Jesus proclaims:

> *You invalidated the word of God for the sake of your tradition. You hypocrites, rightly did Isaiah prophesy of you: 'This people honors me with their lips, but their heart is far away from me. 'But in vain do they worship me, teaching as doctrines the precepts of men.' (Matthew 15:6b-9)*

---

[15] Richard Benton and Marc Boulos, "Consumer or Consumed," *The Bible as Literature*, podcast audio, February 2014. www.hipcast.com/podcast/Hf5vbCgQ

31

Biblical Pedagogy

Like Nathan, the Bible constantly challenges our pieties with stories that illustrate the true, complex nature of our behavior. Its examples are painful, socially inappropriate, and often violent precisely because they reflect the painful, socially inappropriate and violent nature of human behavior. The universality of the Bible's narrative compels us to see our reflection in the folly of its characters.

We filter the Bible for the same reason that we condemn others: because we do not want to face the truth about ourselves. We soften the Bible's edges with gentle words because we hope to be seen—on the basis of appearance—as good pastors. Yet, we know from the prophet Jeremiah that human words are deceptive (Jeremiah 7:4). Just as Twain's censors obfuscate his blatant presentation of American history, we construct ideologies for the Bible that allow us to avoid its teaching, hiding from our own hypocrisy in order to lift ourselves up. Our sanitized, self-effacing piety is but whitewash over the most heinous human behavior of all: the supplanting of God's teaching with human words, as if man is himself a god. Truly, human judgment is the purest form of self-delusion.

Only the Bible can dismantle the stubborn edifice of human self-righteousness. God forbid the student imitate the "good" teacher (or the parishioner the "holy" priest) propagating pious arrogance. Human teachers, like all students, are inescapably hypocritical, "so practice and observe whatever they tell you," Jesus said, "but not what they do (Matthew 23:3)." As such, the teacher must be removed from the equation, so that the biblical teaching can work directly on the human conscience. Only then can the Bible propagate life for Israel and the nations. So what is the role of the teacher? To repeat the teaching. As the Good Book says:

> *When your son asks you in time to come, saying, 'What do the testimonies and the statutes and the judgments mean which the Lord our God commanded you?' Then you shall say to your son, 'We were slaves to Pharaoh in Egypt, and the Lord brought us from Egypt with a mighty hand. Moreover, the Lord showed great and distressing signs and wonders before our eyes against Egypt, Pharaoh and all his household; He brought us out from there in order to bring us in, to give us the land which he had sworn to our fathers.' So the Lord commanded us to observe all these statutes, to fear the Lord our God for our good always and for our survival, as it is today. (Deuteronomy 6:20–24)*

Such is the letter to the Galatians. More an expository sermon than a commentary, this book too is repetitive, since it follows the structure of Paul's epistle as closely as possible.

The Anti-Idolatry School

"Cato, who meanwhile had been left in charge of Utica, despaired of further resistance. With a philosophic composure which befitted his Stoic professions, he first read and then re-read Plato's celebrated dialogue on the immortality of the soul, then drew his sword and stabbed himself mortally in the breast. He was not a great man."

—*Cyril Robinson*[16]

There is a serious problem with the reaction of Christians to the biblical concept of God's will. Straying from the writings of Paul, which identify the will of God as the content of the Bible,[17] Christians tend to imagine a god who communicates his will by speaking with them directly. This tendency contradicts the intent of scripture, in which God's will is handed down as a legally binding text. This text is given to expose the fraudulence of anyone who would dare speak on God's behalf. Paul stresses this point with an analogy:

> *To give a human example, brethren: no one annuls even a man's will, or adds to it, once it has been ratified. (Galatians 3:15)*

---

[16] Cyril E. Robinson, *A History of the Roman Republic* (London: Thomas Y. Crowell Company Publishers, 1932), 408.

[17] D. Francois Tolmie, *Persuading the Galatians: A text-centered Analysis of a Pauline Letter* (Tübingen, Germany: Mohr Siebeck, 2005), 124, 129. The content of God's will was spoken to Abraham in the story of Genesis. Like the text of a human will, the canonical text of Genesis is immutable.

If even a human will is immutable, he explains, how could anyone deviate from the content of the Older Testament? In reality, religious adherents of all kinds routinely break with God's will, ascribing human desires and words to him that have little or no relation to the text of the Bible. When engaged in conflict with our spouse, we know what the Bible demands of us, yet we pray to "discern" God's will, as if our prayer will cause scripture to rewrite itself. Finally, we either submit to our spouse *as instructed,* or justify another course of action under the guise of prayer. Like teenagers in love with our idea of someone, we abuse prayer as an occasion to create an *idea* of our personal god. We then place this god on a pedestal and use it to advance our private agenda. This type of god—the projection of human thought—typifies the biblical concept of an idol. In the Older Testament, the statues and temples deemed "idols" by the prophets are but metaphors for the commonplace ritual of self-worship, in which human beings place something of human origin on a divine pedestal.

In the New Testament, the Bible's critique of this behavior plays out in Paul's examination of circumcision and the works of the Law. The church in Jerusalem had enshrined its traditions, religious identity, and liturgical customs as a kind of god. In turn, Paul applied the Torah to the church, making an example of Jerusalem by condemning its religious teachings and piety as *works of the flesh.* In the Bible, the word *flesh* refers to anything of human or temporal origin. Enthroned under the guise of

Jesus Christ, this false god, fashioned by Jerusalem's hand, became a vehicle of power for church leaders.

In opposition to the "Pillars"[19] of Jerusalem (Galatians 2:9; Peter, James and John), in Galatians, Paul argued that the biblical polemic against idolatry found its full expression, not in religious piety and its achievements, but in the crucifixion of Jesus. While human gods, like Jerusalem's leaders, glory in their own strength, the biblical God is glorified in human weakness. By submitting to death on the cross, Jesus, the anti-idol, personally embodied the death of humanity's gods. That anyone, let alone the church, would advance their own power in the name of Jesus was totally unacceptable to Paul. The biblical concept of Jesus as anti-god, which posed a genuine threat to the religious elite in Jerusalem, was no less controversial for Roman society.

As a military state, the Romans found the Pauline concept of a crucified messiah dangerous and irrational. Where Roman culture idolized strength and honor, the cross typified weakness and shame.[20] A true god, one with Caesar's power and social status, would never have allowed his enemies to execute him. To apply the imperial titles, "Son of the Gods" and "Savior of Rome," to Jesus was not

---

[19] I am indebted to David Pates, who points out the link between the pejorative title "Pillars" and temple architecture.

[20] J.E. Lendon, *Empire of Honour: The Art of Government in the Roman World* (New York: Oxford University Press, 1997), 243.

only treasonous, but idiotic.[21] So incompatible was the death of Jesus with pagan concepts of divinity that St. Justin Martyr, a Palestinian writer and apologist from the second century, was forced to explain that Christians were not atheists:

> *Hence are we called atheists, and we confess that we are atheists, so far as gods of this sort are concerned, but not with respect to the most true God… (First Apologia, Chapter VI)[22]*

The teaching of Jesus was construed as atheism because the Romans recognized, correctly, that the death of Jesus meant the death of their gods, the end of their religion, and the decline of Roman power. It should come as no surprise, then, that Roman law prohibited any god "not made by human hands" and sanctioned by the Senate.[23]

In both communities—Jerusalem and Rome—the claim of divine power was predicated on the promise that those in positions of authority could provide security. Insofar as human strength is transitory, whether religious or political in nature, Paul considered these promises false and manipulative. How could an emperor or a priest, having no control over his own life, guarantee life for anyone else? This limitation is stressed by the metaphor of

---

[21] Robert Forman Hortman, *A History of the Romans* (London: Longmans, Green and Co., 1891), 313.

[22] Leslie W. Barnard, *The First and Second Apologies* (New Jersey: Paulist Press, 1997), 26.

[23] Edith Bramhall and Dana Munro, *The Early Christian Persecutions* (Philadelphia: University of Pennsylvania, 1913), 3.

the empty tomb in the gospels, which, like the tree of life in Genesis, sets a clear boundary between humanity and the power of life (Genesis 3:24). Previously, Egyptian civilization made similar claims, using the promise of eternal life to consolidate Pharaoh's ascendancy over his subjects. In the coercive ritual of living burials, Egyptian religion offered its slaves no escape from the horrors of Pharaoh's tyranny, even in death.[24]

While it is true that no human authority has the power to give life, the illusion of power is easily maintained by threatening to *harm* life. In effect, a king or priest manufactures a crisis and then presents himself as the solution. Paul termed this pattern of behavior "the power of death," noting its systematic dependence on the agency of fear (Hebrews 2:14–15). In opposition to this power, the gospel of Jesus Christ sought to "free those who through fear of death were subject to slavery all their lives," by supplanting the fear of temporary humans with that of

---

[24] Sir Ernest A.W. Budge, *Osiris and the Egyptian Resurrection, Volume 1* (London: Philip Lee Warner, 1911), xxii. "Egyptians were in the habit of burying slaves alive in the graves of great kings and chiefs, so that their spirits might depart to their masters in the Other World, and minister to their souls there as they had ministered to the needs of their bodies upon earth. A vignette in the Book 'Am-Tuat' even suggests that slaves had been buried alive in the tomb, one at each of the four corners, which held the mortal body of Osiris."

the permanent God.[25] In Jesus' own words:

> *Do not fear those who kill the body but are unable to kill the soul; but rather fear him who is able to destroy both soul and body in hell. (Matthew 10:28)* [26]

Indeed, the horrid practice of burying Egyptian slaves alive is reversed in liturgical accounts of Christ's decent into hell, where Jesus is said to have "loosed the bonds of those held captive."[27]

It is into this oppressive setting, historical and religious, that Paul introduced his letter to the Galatians, a succinct but rigorous exposition of the teaching of the Older Testament. Through his careful application of the Torah, Paul exposed Jerusalem's fatal misreading of biblical circumcision: a practice given to remove social barriers had been co-opted to build the same.

Writing to reestablish the authority of the Bible in Galatia, Paul pleaded with his disciples to choose the gospel, which comes from God, over the authority of church leaders. Where God's teaching strove to liberate the Galatians from their human masters, the latter co-opted scripture to impose their religious teachings and identity. In so doing, the Pillars had betrayed the Torah,

---

[25] "The fear of the Lord is a fountain of life, that one may avoid the snares of death." (Proverbs 14:27; Hebrews 2:15)

[26] See Proverbs 1–2. To fear God is to follow the wisdom of his teaching.

[27] Isabel Hapgood, *Service Book of the Holy Orthodox-Catholic Apostolic (Greco-Russian) Church* (Cambridge: The Riverside Press, 1906), 448.

preaching things that pass away as though they were eternal. Worse, they had done so at the expense of the weaker brother, even after publicly affirming their acceptance of Paul's gospel.

In a commanding exposition of Genesis, Paul undermined Jerusalem's idolatry by proclaiming the meaning of Christ's resurrection: *only* the Lord, who made the heavens and the earth, has the power to bestow life and to safeguard its continuation.

Like Jerusalem, the gentiles in Galatia had embraced the delusional belief that the work of their own hands could raise the dead. In turn, Paul argued zealously that the Galatians were fools to choose the authority of men (the flesh) over the content of God's written teaching (the Spirit). Ignoring the death of Jesus, which undermines human virtue, the Galatians looked to religious piety as their source of life. Paul countered by stating the obvious: no matter how hard human beings strive, they cannot outrun their death through ritual bribery. This fact is explicated by his discussion of Deuteronomy's curses, in which he demonstrates the futility of human askesis (Galatians 3:10).

Faced with the tyranny of Rome and a religious ideology intent upon its own power, Paul preached the counter-intuitive God of the Bible: a deity lacking form and power in human eyes, through whom *every* human form and power is destroyed. It is *this* God, incarnate in the pages of Paul's letter, who alone wields the power of life.

"Hold thy peace, O Orpheus; Hermes, cast aside thy lyre. The tripod at Delphi does sink into oblivion hereafter. For David playeth for us the lyre of the Spirit."[28]

[28] Michael Asser, *The Psalter of the Prophet and King David With the Nine Biblical Odes* (Etna, California: CTOS Press, St. Gregory Palamas Monastery, 2008), 11.

Chapter 1

Not From Men

"Cursed is the man who trusts in mankind and makes flesh his strength, and whose heart turns away from the Lord."
(Jeremiah 17:5)

Galatians 1:1–2

1:1 Paul an apostle—not from men nor through man, but through Jesus Christ and God the Father, who raised him from the dead —2 and all the brethren who are with me, to the churches of Galatia:

1:1 Παῦλος, ἀπόστολος οὐκ ἀπ᾽ ἀνθρώπων, οὐδὲ δι᾽ ἀνθρώπου, ἀλλὰ διὰ Ἰησοῦ Χριστοῦ καὶ Θεοῦ πατρὸς τοῦ ἐγείραντος αὐτὸν ἐκ νεκρῶν, 2 καὶ οἱ σὺν ἐμοὶ πάντες ἀδελφοί, ταῖς ἐκκλησίαις τῆς Γαλατίας·

U.S. Supreme Court Justice, Stephen Breyer, was interviewed about the problem of political ideology in the court system. During the interview, he explained that once a written decision of the court is ratified, no one is permitted to contradict it:

When I speak of an opinion I wrote, as I do sometimes, I'm not going beyond what I wrote. Moreover, when I remember what I wrote and I have said something that isn't in the opinion, what I say does not count. What counts is what is written. Little commentaries on that after—no matter how

> *they try to keep to the opinion—may sometimes stray, and if*
> *they stray, they're wrong.*[29]

For Breyer, it is the *written* decision of the court, not its authors or interpreters, that holds authority. This attempts to ensure that no individual or group—not even the author of the ruling—may impose their personal will on others. By analogy, Breyer's comments help illustrate Paul's claim that the letter to the Galatians is "not from men" (1:1).[30]

Unlike wise men and elders common to all religions, the Apostle Paul never presents himself as one having authority stemming from personal wisdom, affiliation, or experience. On the contrary, when Paul chooses to speak of his achievements, they are cast in a negative light.[31] Boasting, he explains, is necessary for instructing the worldly; aside from this, it has no advantage before God (2 Corinthians 11–12:1). Where other apostles sought distinction through their ephemeral relationship with Jesus (1:19), in Galatians, Paul's apostleship is linked solely to his commission, given through Jesus Christ "and God the Father" (1:1). The latter's inclusion is critical, since it was the Father's "will" (1:4) to raise Jesus from the dead. If Paul were to bring this life to the nations, his

---

[29] Stephen Breyer, "Inside the Supreme Court," *Word for Word*, 2007, wordforword.publicradio.org/programs/2007/09/28/ (28 September 2007).
[30] References to Galatians throughout the rest of this book are presented with chapter and verse numbers only.
[31] Paul refers to his own boasting as "foolishness" (2 Corinthians 11:1).

authority had to come from the same progenitor, since anything of human origin is passing away. Paul's commission to preach the word was assigned by the living God (1:1; 1:15–16) in *contempt* of worldly pedigree, as were the biblical prophets:

> *Now the word of the Lord came to me saying, 'Before I formed you in the womb I knew you, and before you were born I consecrated you; I have appointed you a prophet to the nations.' Then I said, 'Alas, Lord God! Behold, I do not know how to speak, because I am a youth.' But the Lord said to me, 'Do not say, 'I am a youth,' because everywhere I send you, you shall go, and all that I command you, you shall speak. Do not be afraid of them, for I am with you to deliver you,' declares the Lord. (Jeremiah 1:4–8)*

As in the case of Jeremiah, an inexperienced youth, Paul had no personal credibility with his audience. He was a persecutor of the church, "the least" of all the Lord's people (Ephesians 3:8) and the last person to be received as an apostle.

Throughout scripture, there are instances in which God seems to choose his favorites arbitrarily. Other times, he chooses the least likely: Abel, with no indication that Cain's offering was deficient (Genesis 4:1–5); Sarah, despite her abuse of Hagar (Genesis 16:6); and Jacob, who conspired with his wicked mother to cheat Esau of his inheritance (Genesis 27:18–19). None of these characters stand on their own merits. On the contrary, they were chosen by the will of God; for Paul, it is this *will*, not the individual characters, that is worthy of boasting.[32] The same informs and directs its messengers "everywhere" it pleases, according to its own purpose. Just as Jeremiah, beginning with Jerusalem, was sent to proclaim God's instruction "to the nations," Paul was sent to the church. It is important to note that Jeremiah did not bring anything new. His commission was to remind Judah of God's original written instruction, which they had rejected at great peril (Jeremiah 6:19). Paul's claim that his apostleship was "not from men" was to reassert the authority of the very same teaching over himself, the other apostles, and the addressees of his letter. That this teaching was now open to the gentile community was a reflection of God's grace (1:3) in fulfillment of Jeremiah's mission, since through Jesus Christ, all social and ideological barriers separating the nations from Abraham's household had been overcome.

Galatians 1:3–5

3 Grace to you and peace from God the Father and our Lord Jesus Christ, 4 who gave himself for our sins to deliver us from

---

[32] "But if you bear the name 'Jew' and rely upon the Law and boast in God, and know his will and approve the things that are essential, being instructed out of the Law, and are confident that you yourself are a guide to the blind, a light to those who are in darkness, a corrector of the foolish, a teacher of the immature, having in the Law the embodiment of knowledge and of the truth, you, therefore, who teach another, do you not teach yourself?" (Romans 2:17–21)

*the present evil age, according to the will of our God and
Father; 5 to whom be the glory forever and ever. Amen.*

*3 χάρις ὑμῖν καὶ εἰρήνη ἀπὸ Θεοῦ πατρὸς καὶ Κυρίου ἡμῶν
Ἰησοῦ Χριστοῦ, 4 τοῦ δόντος ἑαυτὸν ὑπὲρ τῶν ἁμαρτιῶν
ἡμῶν, ὅπως ἐξέληται ἡμᾶς ἐκ τοῦ ἐνεστῶτος αἰῶνος πονηροῦ
κατὰ τὸ θέλημα τοῦ Θεοῦ καὶ πατρὸς ἡμῶν, 5 ᾧ ἡ δόξα εἰς
τοὺς αἰῶνας τῶν αἰώνων· ἀμήν*

The words "grace" and "peace" (1:3) are the traditional
seal of Paul's letters.[33] The day of grace is a metaphor for
the first hearing of the gospel, in this example, the
beginning of the letter itself.[34] The day of peace is a day
in the future when the reader will be judged as to how they
acted on this grace.[35] In this sense, the word *peace* is
eschatological: it deals with the end of history, when the
resurrected Lord will appear in judgment. In practical
terms, the day of peace is a euphemism for the reader's
death.[36] Until that day comes, Jesus' followers must
endure the "present evil age" (1:4) dominated by false
kings and empires. In Paul's specific historical context, the
evil age is an allusion to Roman tyranny.

In the Older Testament, God offers his people an

---

[33] Paul Nadim Tarazi, *Volume 45: Romans, Orthodox Audio Bible
Commentary* (St. Paul, Minnesota: OCABS Press, 2004).

[34] See Colossians 1: 5-6.

[35] Tarazi, *Volume 45: Romans, Orthodox Audio Bible Commentary.*

[36] William John Copeland, *Commentary on Galatians and Homilies on
Ephesians by St. John Chrysostom* (London: J.G.F. and J Rivington, 1840),
368. Compare 1 Thessalonians 5:2 and Matthew 24:42-44. Like death, the
day of the Lord is unpredictable and comes without warning.

alternative to the cyclical tyranny of human monarchs by proposing an everlasting kingdom ruled by God himself (ex. 1 Samuel 8). It is to this kingdom that Paul is committed, wherein "nation will not lift up sword against nation, and men will never again learn war" (Isaiah 2:4). In Isaiah, this new dominion is to include all the nations of the earth (Isaiah 2:3). In keeping with this promise, Paul's letter was written to extend God's offer of kingship to the Roman Empire, and beyond.

As a first century Jew, Paul was surrounded by ideologues intent upon revolution against Rome. This spirit found its tragic fulfillment in the Jewish Revolt and subsequent destruction of the Temple in 70 AD. In contrast, Paul considered himself a citizen of God's coming kingdom, in which the "glory" of victory is "forever" consigned to God the Father (1:5), beyond the reach of human hands. According to Isaiah, under the dominion of God's Torah, the peoples of the earth will one day "hammer their swords into plowshares and their spears into pruning hooks" (Isaiah 2:4). For Paul, it is the promise of this kingdom that is the true patrimony of the circumcised. As such, the Romans were to be embraced, not attacked.

Galatians 1:6–9

6 I am astonished that you are so quickly deserting him who called you in the grace of Christ and turning to a different gospel — 7 not that there is another gospel, but there are some who trouble you and want to pervert the gospel of Christ. 8 But even if we, or an angel from heaven, should preach to you a gospel contrary to that which we preached to you, let him be accursed. 9 As we have said before, so now I say again, if anyone is preaching to you a gospel contrary to that which you received, let him be accursed.

6 Θαυμάζω ὅτι οὕτω ταχέως μετατίθεσθε ἀπὸ τοῦ καλέσαντος ὑμᾶς ἐν χάριτι Χριστοῦ εἰς ἕτερον εὐαγγέλιον, 7 ὃ οὐκ ἔστιν ἄλλο, εἰ μὴ τινές εἰσιν οἱ ταράσσοντες ὑμᾶς καὶ θέλοντες μεταστρέψαι τὸ εὐαγγέλιον τοῦ Χριστοῦ 8 ἀλλὰ καὶ ἐὰν ἡμεῖς ἢ ἄγγελος ἐξ οὐρανοῦ εὐαγγελίζηται ὑμῖν παρ' ὃ εὐηγγελισάμεθα ὑμῖν, ἀνάθεμα ἔστω 9 ὡς προειρήκαμεν, καὶ ἄρτι πάλιν λέγω· εἴ τις ὑμᾶς εὐαγγελίζεται παρ' ὃ παρελάβετε, ἀνάθεμα ἔστω

Where "the grace of Christ" (1:6) has waived all social barriers to participation in God's kingdom, Paul's opponents "want to pervert the gospel of Christ" (1:7) by imposing their religious identity on the Galatians through the ritual act of circumcision, a topic that will be covered at length. With hyperbole akin to Breyer's comments, Paul insists that even God himself (through his angel) may not contradict what is written in Galatians, namely, the gospel he previously laid before them (1:8). To contradict this teaching is to render oneself accursed, in the original Greek, *anáthema* (ἀνάθεμα): a person or thing devoted to destruction, typically, as a religious offering.[37] The term's usage is poignant, since within the letter's framework, deviation from the "spiritual" rule of scripture through religious practices consigns one to destruction with the

---

[37] See Numbers 21:3, Leviticus 27:28, Deuteronomy 7:26; 13:16.

Not From Men

flesh, itself fated to the dust from which it was taken (5:2; 6:8).

The Power of Death

Galatians 1:10–14

10 Am I now seeking the favor of men, or of God? Or am I trying to please men? If I were still pleasing men, I should not be a servant of Christ. 11 For I would have you know, brethren, that the gospel which was preached by me is not man's gospel. 12 For I did not receive it from man, nor was I taught it, but it came through a revelation of Jesus Christ. 13 For you have heard of my former life in Judaism, how I persecuted the church of God violently and tried to destroy it; 14 and I advanced in Judaism beyond many of my own age among my people, so extremely zealous was I for the traditions of my fathers.

10 ἄρτι γὰρ ἀνθρώπους πείθω ἢ τὸν Θεόν; ἢ ζητῶ ἀνθρώποις ἀρέσκειν; εἰ γὰρ ἔτι ἀνθρώποις ἤρεσκον, Χριστοῦ δοῦλος οὐκ ἂν ἤμην 11 Γνωρίζω δὲ ὑμῖν, ἀδελφοί, τὸ εὐαγγέλιον τὸ εὐαγγελισθὲν ὑπ' ἐμοῦ ὅτι οὐκ ἔστι κατὰ ἄνθρωπον· 12 οὐδὲ γὰρ ἐγὼ παρὰ ἀνθρώπου παρέλαβον αὐτὸ οὔτε ἐδιδάχθην, ἀλλὰ δι' ἀποκαλύψεως Ἰησοῦ Χριστοῦ 13 Ἠκούσατε γὰρ τὴν ἐμὴν ἀναστροφήν ποτε ἐν τῷ Ἰουδαϊσμῷ, ὅτι καθ' ὑπερβολὴν ἐδίωκον τὴν ἐκκλησίαν τοῦ Θεοῦ καὶ ἐπόρθουν αὐτήν, 14 καὶ προέκοπτον ἐν τῷ Ἰουδαϊσμῷ ὑπὲρ πολλοὺς συνηλικιώτας ἐν τῷ γένει μου, περισσοτέρως ζηλωτὴς ὑπάρχων τῶν πατρικῶν μου παραδόσεων

If Paul were to seek "the favor of men" or attempt "to please men" in any way, he would immediately forfeit his status as a slave of Jesus Christ (1:10). "No one," Jesus explained, "can serve two masters" (Matthew 6:24). Since

Paul answers only to God (1:11–12), in his first visit to Jerusalem (1:18) he did not seek the approval of the other apostles, only their submission to the grace of the gospel.

In general, people seek "the favor of men" in order to establish position and power.[38] An individual does so by playing on the desire of others for permanence and security. Such control is eagerly given, since people "ascribe power to [those] who achieve their objectives."[39] In reality, nothing is permanent except God:

> *You, Lord, in the beginning laid the foundation of the earth and the heavens are the works of your hands; they will perish, but you remain; and they all will become old like a garment and like a mantle you will roll them up; like a garment they will also be changed. But you are the same and your years will not come to an end. (Psalm 102: 25–27; Hebrews 1:11–12)*

> *The gods that did not make the heavens and the earth will perish from the earth and from under the heavens. (Jeremiah 10:11)*

When a group forsakes God, "who laid the foundation of the earth," by placing its trust in the illusion of human strength, Paul describes this deception elsewhere as "the power of death" (Hebrews 2:14). Such a group transfers authority to an individual in the hope of achieving something temporary as though it were permanent. In

---

[38] Antonius H. N. Cillessen, David Schwartz, and Lara Mayeux, *Popularity in the Peer System* (New York: Guilford Press, 2011), 12.
[39] Ibid., 16.

reality, this individual, their provision for others, and the "earth" on which their group resides will all "come to an end." In Paul's historical context, the power of death was wielded by the "divine" emperor of Rome, who exercised authority over life and death in the arena.[40] In Hebrews, this death is akin to the bondage in Egypt, from which God rescued the children of Abraham.[41]

Rooted in fear, power of this type is easily transferred to the many gods that dominate human affairs: rulers, nations, ideologies, institutions, and (in Galatians) religious identity and its corresponding rituals (1:14). In truth, human beings are powerless over their own fates, unable to "make even one hair white or black" (Matthew 5:36). "You would have no authority over me," Jesus warned Pontius Pilate, "unless it had been given you from above" (John 19:11). Although Pilate had no control, he was able to maintain the illusion of power because the mob did not yet see that God would "put all things in subjection under [Jesus'] feet" (1 Corinthians 15:27). Paul's violent behavior on behalf of his own religious group illustrates these themes.

Like all violence, Paul's persecution of the church (1:13) grew in response to his own group's demand for security.

---

[40] Paul Nadim Tarazi, *The Chrysostom Bible – Hebrews: A Commentary* (St. Paul, Minnesota: OCABS Press, 2014), 50.
[41] Ibid., 51.

Demarcation between Jews and gentiles was a central tenet of Jewish nationalism leading up to the Temple Revolt.[42] In blurring the lines of social identity, the followers of Jesus posed a genuine threat to Jewish homogeneity.[43] Far from popular, Paul's turnabout inclusion of the uncircumcised ensured life for the nations, but estrangement from his own family. "A prophet," Jesus explained, "is not without honor except in his own town, among his relatives and in his own household" (Mark 6:4). By seeking the favor of God (1:10), Paul not only forwent his own power, but prevented others from holding power over the Galatians. As such, he found himself outcast with Jesus Christ: the content of his gospel (1:11–12), through whom *only* the Father can provide life for the gentiles. "Heaven and earth will pass away," Jesus said, "but my words will not pass away" (Matthew 24:35).

The First Shall Be Last

Galatians 1:15–24

15 But when he who had set me apart before I was born, and had called me through his grace, 16 was pleased to reveal his Son to me, in order that I might preach him among the Gentiles, I did not confer with flesh and blood, 17 nor did I go up to Jerusalem to those who were apostles before me, but I went away into Arabia; and again I returned to Damascus. 18 Then

---

[42] Brendan Byrne, *Galatians and Romans* (Collegeville, Minnesota: Liturgical Press, 2010), 50.
[43] Ibid.

after three years I went up to Jerusalem to visit Cephas, and remained with him fifteen days. 19 But I saw none of the other apostles except James the Lord's brother. 20 (In what I am writing to you, before God, I do not lie!) 21 Then I went into the regions of Syria and Cilicia. 22 And I was still not known by sight to the churches of Christ in Judea; 23 they only heard it said, "He who once persecuted us is now preaching the faith he once tried to destroy." 24 And they glorified God because of me.

15 Ὅτε δὲ εὐδόκησεν ὁ Θεὸς ὁ ἀφορίσας με ἐκ κοιλίας μητρός μου καὶ καλέσας διὰ τῆς χάριτος αὐτοῦ 16 ἀποκαλύψαι τὸν υἱὸν αὐτοῦ ἐν ἐμοί, ἵνα εὐαγγελίζωμαι αὐτὸν ἐν τοῖς ἔθνεσιν, εὐθέως οὐ προσανεθέμην σαρκὶ καὶ αἵματι, 17 οὐδὲ ἀνῆλθον εἰς Ἱεροσόλυμα πρὸς τοὺς πρὸ ἐμοῦ ἀποστόλους, ἀλλὰ ἀπῆλθον εἰς Ἀραβίαν, καὶ πάλιν ὑπέστρεψα εἰς Δαμασκόν 18 Ἔπειτα μετὰ ἔτη τρία ἀνῆλθον εἰς Ἱεροσόλυμα ἱστορῆσαι Πέτρον, καὶ ἐπέμεινα πρὸς αὐτὸν ἡμέρας δεκαπέντε· 19 ἕτερον δὲ τῶν ἀποστόλων οὐκ εἶδον εἰ μὴ Ἰάκωβον τὸν ἀδελφὸν τοῦ Κυρίου 20 ἃ δὲ γράφω ὑμῖν, ἰδοὺ ἐνώπιον τοῦ Θεοῦ ὅτι οὐ ψεύδομαι 21 ἔπειτα ἦλθον εἰς τὰ κλίματα τῆς Συρίας καὶ τῆς Κιλικίας 22 ἤμην δὲ ἀγνοούμενος τῷ προσώπῳ ταῖς ἐκκλησίαις τῆς Ἰουδαίας ταῖς ἐν Χριστῷ· 23 μόνον δὲ ἀκούοντες ἦσαν ὅτι ὁ διώκων ἡμᾶς ποτε νῦν εὐαγγελίζεται τὴν πίστιν ἥν ποτε ἐπόρθει, 24 καὶ ἐδόξαζον ἐν ἐμοὶ τὸν Θεόν

Paul's emphasis, that he "did not confer with flesh and blood" (1:16) and did not "go up to Jerusalem" underscores his earlier assertion, that his commission was received directly from God (1:1), with no input from the other apostles (1:17). Under divine commission, after a period of "three years," Paul "went up to Jerusalem" with the gospel, visiting Peter (Cephas) and James (1:18–19) for the first time; in effect, Jerusalem's day of grace. Paul's review of his first encounter lays the groundwork for a discussion of the second visit, which took place during the council at Jerusalem.

The Acts of the Apostles offers a detailed account of the council, where both Peter and James publicly endorsed Paul's teaching, agreeing that gentiles need not be circumcised as Jews in order to follow Jesus. In Galatians, however, Paul shows that Peter and James condemned themselves in their testimonies (Acts 15:4–20). Both men jeopardized Paul's ministry by turning their backs on promises made at the meeting.[44] This point is emphasized in Paul's account of the resurrection in 1 Corinthians. There too, Paul is dismayed by the church's rejection of the gospel it formerly embraced:

> *Now I make known to you, brethren, the gospel which I preached to you, which also you received, in which also you stand, by which also you are saved, if you hold fast the word which I preached to you, unless you believed in vain. I delivered to you as of first importance what I also received, that Christ died for our sins according to the Scriptures, and that he was buried, and that he was raised on the third day according to the Scriptures, and that he appeared to Cephas, then to the twelve. After that he appeared to more than five hundred brethren at one time, most of whom remain until now, but some have fallen asleep; then he appeared to James,*

---

[44] Immediately following the council, Paul and Barnabas traveled to Antioch (2:1-10; Acts 15:30) where the betrayal took place (2:11–3).

*then to all the apostles; and last of all, as to one untimely
born, he appeared to me also. For I am the least of the apostles,
and not fit to be called an apostle, because I persecuted the
church of God. (1 Corinthians 15:1–9)*

The story of Christ's appearances following his
resurrection in 1 Corinthians parallel the account of Paul's
first visit to Jerusalem (1:18). The apostle's conversion on
the road to Damascus (Acts 9:4), his baptism (Acts 9:18),
and "three year" sojourn abroad are all metaphors for his
death. After "three years" (1:18) alluding to Jesus' three
days in the tomb, Paul appeared first to Cephas, and later,
James. In 1 Corinthians, Paul uses this parallelism to
subtly align the coming of Christ with his initial delivery
of the gospel to Jerusalem.

If Paul is considered the "least of the apostles" (1
Corinthians 15:9) he is the closest to Jesus, whose
shameful death belittled him in the eyes of Rome and
Jerusalem. Paul's observation, "that he was not known by
sight" (1:22), and was "only heard" in Judea (1:23),
emphasizes this association, since those searching the
empty tomb find nothing but a word from the angel; a
deity with no effigy (Luke 24:7–8; Mark 16:6–7). It is
only through this word that Jerusalem "glorifies God"
(1:24). Paul's claim, that they "glorified God" because of
him, denotes Jerusalem's initial acceptance of the gospel.
Far from boasting, this claim defers to the Father of Jesus,
whose will set Paul apart from others (1:15), providing the
content of the gospel and the commission to carry it to the
nations.

Conversely, having received the worldly honor of being first, Peter is the *greatest* of the apostles, and the one most alienated from the crucified Lord. James too, "the brother of the Lord" (1:19), is given more ephemeral honor than the other apostles (1 Corinthians 15:7). It is ominous that Jesus appeared to Peter first, since the day of the Lord's appearing is a day of reckoning (John 5:25–29). Now that the gospel has graced Peter and James, its content will soon judge them.

Chapter 2

Circumcision

"All the nations are uncircumcised, and all the house of Israel are uncircumcised of heart." (Jeremiah 9:26b)

A Lion Has Gone up from His Thicket

Galatians 2:1–13

2:1 Then after fourteen years I went up again to Jerusalem with Barnabas, taking Titus along with me. 2 I went up by revelation; and I laid before them (but privately before those who were of repute) the gospel which I preach among the Gentiles, lest somehow I should be running or had run in vain. 3 But even Titus, who was with me, was not compelled to be circumcised, though he was a Greek. 4 But because of false brethren secretly brought in, who slipped in to spy out our freedom which we have in Christ Jesus, that they might bring us into bondage — 5 to them we did not yield submission even for a moment, that the truth of the gospel might be preserved for you. 6 And from those who were reputed to be something (what they were makes no difference to me; God shows no partiality) — those, I say, who were of repute added nothing to me; 7 but on the contrary, when they saw that I had been entrusted with the gospel to the uncircumcised, just as Peter had been entrusted with the gospel to the circumcised 8 (for he who worked through Peter for the mission to the circumcised worked through me also for the Gentiles), 9 and when they perceived the grace that was given to me, James and Cephas and John, who were reputed to be pillars, gave to me and Barnabas the right hand of fellowship, that we should go to the Gentiles and they to the circumcised; 10 only they would have us remember the poor, which very thing I was eager to do. 11 But when Cephas came to Antioch I opposed him to his face, because he stood condemned. 12 For before certain men came from James, he ate with the Gentiles; but when they came he drew back and separated himself, fearing the circumcision party. 13 And with him the rest of the Jews acted insincerely, so that even Barnabas was carried away by their insincerity.

2:1 Ἔπειτα διὰ δεκατεσσάρων ἐτῶν πάλιν ἀνέβην εἰς Ἱεροσόλυμα μετὰ Βαρνάβα, συμπαραλαβὼν καὶ Τίτον· 2 ἀνέβην δὲ κατὰ ἀποκάλυψιν· καὶ ἀνεθέμην αὐτοῖς τὸ εὐαγγέλιον ὃ κηρύσσω ἐν τοῖς ἔθνεσι, κατ᾽ ἰδίαν δὲ τοῖς δοκοῦσι, μήπως εἰς κενὸν τρέχω ἢ ἔδραμον 3 ἀλλ᾽ οὐδὲ Τίτος ὁ σὺν ἐμοί, Ἕλλην ὤν, ἠναγκάσθη περιτμηθῆναι, 4 διὰ δὲ τοὺς παρεισάκτους ψευδαδέλφους, οἵτινες παρεισῆλθον κατασκοπῆσαι τὴν ἐλευθερίαν ἡμῶν ἣν ἔχομεν ἐν Χριστῷ Ἰησοῦ, ἵνα ἡμᾶς καταδουλώσωνται· 5 οἷς οὐδὲ πρὸς ὥραν εἴξαμεν τῇ ὑποταγῇ, ἵνα ἡ ἀλήθεια τοῦ εὐαγγελίου διαμείνῃ πρὸς ὑμᾶς 6 ἀπὸ δὲ τῶν δοκούντων εἶναί τι, ὁποῖοί ποτε ἦσαν οὐδέν μοι διαφέρει· πρόσωπον Θεὸς ἀνθρώπου οὐ λαμβάνει· ἐμοὶ γὰρ οἱ δοκοῦντες οὐδὲν προσανέθεντο, 7 ἀλλὰ τοὐναντίον ἰδόντες ὅτι πεπίστευμαι τὸ εὐαγγέλιον τῆς ἀκροβυστίας καθὼς Πέτρος τῆς περιτομῆς· 8 ὁ γὰρ ἐνεργήσας Πέτρῳ εἰς ἀποστολὴν τῆς περιτομῆς ἐνήργησε καὶ ἐμοὶ εἰς τὰ ἔθνη· 9 καὶ γνόντες τὴν χάριν τὴν δοθεῖσάν μοι, Ἰάκωβος καὶ Κηφᾶς καὶ Ἰωάννης, οἱ δοκοῦντες στῦλοι εἶναι, δεξιὰς ἔδωκαν ἐμοὶ καὶ Βαρνάβᾳ κοινωνίας, ἵνα ἡμεῖς εἰς τὰ ἔθνη, αὐτοὶ δὲ εἰς τὴν περιτομήν· 10 μόνον τῶν πτωχῶν ἵνα μνημονεύωμεν, ὃ καὶ ἐσπούδασα αὐτὸ τοῦτο ποιῆσαι 11 Ὅτε δὲ ἦλθε Πέτρος εἰς Ἀντιόχειαν, κατὰ πρόσωπον αὐτῷ ἀντέστην, ὅτι κατεγνωσμένος ἦν 12 πρὸ τοῦ γὰρ ἐλθεῖν τινας ἀπὸ Ἰακώβου μετὰ τῶν ἐθνῶν συνήσθιεν· ὅτε δὲ ἦλθον, ὑπέστελλε καὶ ἀφώριζεν ἑαυτόν, φοβούμενος τοὺς ἐκ

περιτομῆς 13 καὶ συνυπεκρίθησαν αὐτῷ καὶ οἱ λοιποὶ
Ἰουδαῖοι, ὥστε καὶ Βαρνάβας συναπήχθη αὐτῶν τῇ ὑποκρίσει

After fourteen years, Paul "went up by revelation," appearing in Jerusalem for the second time (2:1–2). Paul's coming was to secure the dominion of the Lord's Messiah over the nations, beginning with Israel. Speaking with James and Peter directly but privately, Paul gave "those of repute" (2:2) the opportunity to air their grievances ahead of the Jerusalem council. In line with his disavowal of the "favor of men" (1:10) Paul is explicit in his ambivalence toward their supposed importance (2:6). Note Paul's sarcasm, since who in Jerusalem should be "of repute" other than the Messiah? Following the council, and in contrast with Paul's openness, James and Peter went behind his back, working "secretly" through spies (2:4; 2:12). Worse, they had done so after extending the "right hand of fellowship," (2:9) assuring Paul—privately and publicly—of their acceptance of the gospel to non-Jews.

Knowing that only the Messiah could secure life for his people, Paul continued to insist on the priority of the gospel, that Christ might "continue" or "remain" (διαμένω) for the sake of "the poor," a metaphor for those in need of the Lord's teaching[46] (2:5; 2:10; Jeremiah 5:4).

---

[46] In light of their betrayal of the gospel to the poor, Jerusalem's request that Paul remember the poor calls to mind the *impoverished teacher,* Judas: "But Judas Iscariot, one of his disciples, who was intending to betray him, said,

If his opponents were to reject this teaching, life for both Jew and gentile would be jeopardized and Paul's "running" would have been "in vain" (2:2). By opposing the imposition of circumcision (2:5), Paul was not only questioning Jerusalem's understanding of scripture, but challenging its readiness to put others in harm's way. In the ancient world, circumcision was a dangerous[47] and painful procedure, considered "barbaric and perverse" by Romans.[48] Paul's stubbornness, "not yielding submission even for a moment," was as much an act of mercy as it was insistence on the gospel's primacy (2:5).

That Peter was "entrusted with the gospel to the circumcised" (2:7) does not imply two teachings. On the contrary, for both Jew and gentile, the one gospel of love was given to trample underfoot the tyranny of idolatry. In the Older Testament, the love of God's teaching was prioritized above all other gods (Deuteronomy 6:5) as a prerequisite to the Golden Rule, that the children of Abraham are to love their neighbors as themselves (Leviticus 19:18). For the Jew, that meant embracing the

---

'Why was this perfume not sold for three hundred denarii and given to poor people?' Now he said this, not because he was concerned about the poor, but because he was a thief, and as he had the money box, he used to pilfer what was put into it. Therefore Jesus said, 'Let her alone, so that she may keep it for the day of my burial. For you always have the poor with you, but you do not always have me.'" (John 12:4–8)

[47] Edward Gibbon, *History of the Decline and Fall of the Roman Empire, Volume I* (Cincinnati, Ohio: J.A. James, 1840), 159.

[48] Leland Ryken, et al., *Dictionary of Biblical Imagery: Letter to the Galatians* (Downers Grove, Illinois: InterVarsity Press, 1998), 314.

gentile at the expense of identity; for both, it meant supplanting the "favor of men"—sought by those of repute—with the fear of God's teaching (2:12). This tension plays out in Acts, where the embrace of Paul's ministry is linked to the rejection of Peter's personal glory:

> *When Peter entered, Cornelius met him and fell down at his feet and worshiped him. But Peter lifted him up, saying, 'Stand up; I too am a man.' And as he talked with him, he went in and found many persons gathered; and he said to them, 'You yourselves know how unlawful it is for a Jew to associate with or to visit any one of another nation; but God has shown me that I should not call any man common or unclean.' (Acts 10:25–28)*

Peter's confession that no man should bow down and worship him reflects his original concession to Paul, that to impose one's religious identity on another is to impose one's self. Like his testimony in Jerusalem (Acts 15:7-11), this confession amplifies his betrayal of the gospel. Prior to his visit with Cornelius, Peter received a vision from God instructing him three times to eat unclean foods, since, "What God has cleansed, you must not call common" (Acts 10:15–16). This commandment pertains not to food, but to Peter's fellow human beings. The magnitude of Peter's hypocrisy is dramatized in his betrayal of Jesus. In all four gospels, Peter's denial of Christ—like his vision of unclean foods—is repeated three times (Matthew 26:34; Mark 14:30; Luke 22:61; John 13:38). The "insincerity" of Peter (2:13), who only pretended to live according to strict Jewish practice,[49] is deplorable. Binding burdens on other men's backs that he himself would not carry (Matthew 23:4), Peter "stood condemned" in his use of circumcision as a mechanism of power. Paul had no choice but to oppose him publicly, "to his face" (2:11). "But Peter kept saying, insistently, 'Even if I have to die with you, I will not deny you!'" (Mark 14:31).

In the book of Genesis, the commandment to circumcise underscores the broader theme of the story: 1) that progeny is a gift from God and not an expression of man's greatness;[50] 2) that, beginning with Isaac, each generation of Abraham's children lives because it is produced by God (Genesis 21:1–2; 25:21); and 3) since God is the father of all, Abraham's descendants are to embrace everyone as they would their own people.[51] In the covenant of circumcision, anyone, even foreigners and slaves, can be adopted as children in Abraham's household:

This is my covenant, which you shall keep, between me and you and your descendants after you: every male among you shall be circumcised. And you shall be circumcised in the flesh of your foreskin, and it shall be the sign of the covenant between me and you. And every male among you who is eight

---

[49] Mark J. Edwards, *Galatians, Ephesians, Philippians* (Downers Grove, Illinois: InterVarsity Press, 1999), 26.
[50] Paul Nadim Tarazi, *The Chrysostom Bible – Genesis, A Commentary* (St. Paul, Minnesota: OCABS Press, 2009), 144–45.
[51] Ibid.,150–151.

*days old shall be circumcised throughout your generations, a
servant who is born in the house or who is bought with money
from any foreigner, who is not of your descendants. A servant
who is born in your house or who is bought with your money
shall surely be circumcised; thus shall my covenant be in your
flesh for an everlasting covenant. (Genesis 17:10–13)*

Where circumcision in Genesis emphasizes inclusion
through adoption at will *by God,* [52] for the Pillars, it was
worn as a mark of distinction, establishing tribe and clan
by human hands, in opposition to the nations. This sin is
exposed in the metaphor of Cain's progeny, which
enumerates his rejection of God's will in favor of making
his own children.[53] Like Cain, those of repute in Jerusalem
preferred their own dynasties to children produced by the
spérma (σπέρμα, seed, translated above as "descendants";
Genesis 17:12, LXX) of God's will. In the prophetic
tradition, Jeremiah's implied readers miss this point
entirely:

*'Circumcise yourselves to the Lord, remove the foreskin of your
hearts, O men of Judah and inhabitants of Jerusalem; lest my
wrath go forth like fire, and burn with none to quench it,
because of the evil of your doings.' Declare in Judah, and
proclaim in Jerusalem, and say, 'Blow the trumpet through
the land; cry aloud and say, 'Assemble, and let us go into the
fortified cities!' Raise a standard toward Zion, flee for safety,
stay not, for I bring evil from the north, and great destruction.
A lion has gone up from his thicket, a destroyer of nations has*

---

[52] Ibid.,145.
[53] Ibid., 75.

set out; he has gone forth from his place to make your land a waste; your cities will be ruins without inhabitant. For this gird you with sackcloth, lament and wail; for the fierce anger of the Lord has not turned back from us.' 'In that day,' says the Lord, 'courage shall fail both king and princes; the priests shall be appalled and the prophets astounded.' (Jeremiah 4:1–9; "Foreskin of your hearts," see also: Deuteronomy 10:16, 30:6)

In Jeremiah, to "circumcise the foreskin of the heart" was to change one's behavior toward the foreigner, the orphan, and the widow (Jeremiah 7:4–7), since in the Ancient Near East the heart was considered the seat of intellect, one and the same with a person's manner of living. [54] Where James and Peter used circumcision to magnify the importance of Judaism at the expense of the gentiles, Jeremiah preached circumcision as a call to repentance and a warning of Jerusalem's destruction, should they not change their ways. Poignantly, this destruction was to come "from the north," in the region of Damascus, where Paul received the revelation of Jesus Christ (2:2; Acts 9:3–8).

---

[54] John H. Walton, Victor H. Matthews, and Mark W. Chavalas, *Bible Background Commentary: Old Testament* (Madison, Wisconsin: InterVarsity Press, 1997), 562.

A Broken and Humbled Heart

Galatians 2:14–21

14 But when I saw that they were not straightforward about the truth of the gospel, I said to Cephas before them all, "If you, though a Jew, live like a Gentile and not like a Jew, how can you compel the Gentiles to live like Jews?" 15 We ourselves, who are Jews by birth and not Gentile sinners, 16 yet who know that a man is not justified by works of the Law but through faith in Jesus Christ, even we have believed in Christ Jesus, in order to be justified by faith in Christ, and not by works of the Law, because by works of the Law shall no one be justified. 17 But if, in our endeavor to be justified in Christ, we ourselves were found to be sinners, is Christ then an agent of sin? Certainly not! 18 But if I build up again those things which I tore down, then I prove myself a transgressor. 19 For I through the Law died to the Law, that I might live to God. 20 I have been crucified with Christ; it is no longer I who live, but Christ who lives in me; and the life I now live in the flesh I live by faith in the Son of God, who loved me and gave himself for me. 21 I do not nullify the grace of God; for if justification were through the Law, then Christ died to no purpose.

14 ἀλλ᾽ ὅτε εἶδον ὅτι οὐκ ὀρθοποδοῦσι πρὸς τὴν ἀλήθειαν τοῦ εὐαγγελίου, εἶπον τῷ Πέτρῳ ἔμπροσθεν πάντων· εἰ σὺ Ἰουδαῖος ὑπάρχων ἐθνικῶς ζῇς καὶ οὐκ Ἰουδαϊκῶς, τί τὰ ἔθνη ἀναγκάζεις ἰουδαΐζειν; 15 Ἡμεῖς φύσει Ἰουδαῖοι καὶ οὐκ ἐξ ἐθνῶν ἁμαρτωλοί, 16 εἰδότες δὲ ὅτι οὐ δικαιοῦται ἄνθρωπος ἐξ ἔργων νόμου ἐὰν μὴ διὰ πίστεως Ἰησοῦ Χριστοῦ, καὶ ἡμεῖς εἰς Χριστὸν Ἰησοῦν ἐπιστεύσαμεν, ἵνα δικαιωθῶμεν ἐκ πίστεως Χριστοῦ καὶ οὐκ ἐξ ἔργων νόμου, διότι οὐ δικαιωθήσεται ἐξ ἔργων νόμου πᾶσα σάρξ 17 εἰ δὲ ζητοῦντες δικαιωθῆναι ἐν Χριστῷ εὑρέθημεν καὶ αὐτοὶ ἁμαρτωλοί, ἄρα

Χριστὸς ἁμαρτίας διάκονος; μὴ γένοιτο 18 εἰ γὰρ ἃ κατέλυσα ταῦτα πάλιν οἰκοδομῶ, παραβάτην ἐμαυτὸν συνίστημι 19 ἐγὼ γὰρ διὰ νόμου νόμῳ ἀπέθανον, ἵνα Θεῷ ζήσω 20 Χριστῷ συνεσταύρωμαι· ζῶ δὲ οὐκέτι ἐγώ, ζῇ δὲ ἐν ἐμοὶ Χριστός· ὃ δὲ νῦν ζῶ ἐν σαρκί, ἐν πίστει ζῶ τῇ τοῦ υἱοῦ τοῦ Θεοῦ τοῦ ἀγαπήσαντός με καὶ παραδόντος ἑαυτὸν ὑπὲρ ἐμοῦ 21 Οὐκ ἀθετῶ τὴν χάριν τοῦ Θεοῦ· εἰ γὰρ διὰ νόμου δικαιοσύνη, ἄρα Χριστὸς δωρεὰν ἀπέθανεν

Cutting through Jerusalem's skullduggery, Paul brought the discussion out into the open, holding Peter accountable for his double standard. The accusation that "they were not straightforward about the truth of the gospel" (2:14), was as much a condemnation of Peter's insincerity as it was frustration with his persistent waffling. This is reflected in the use of the term *orthopodéō* (ὀρθοποδέω, straightforward), which literally means "to walk in a straight line," as in, to "walk in my statutes and keep my commandments" (Leviticus 26:3) or to "walk" by the "rule" of the gospel (6:16). For Paul, the "truth of the gospel" (2:14) was not a philosophical concept to be expressed or debated, but a rule of behavior to be followed.[55] "See to it," he explains elsewhere, "that no one takes you captive (συλαγωγῶν, to be made captive of, or to be carried off as prey) through philosophy and empty deception" (Colossians 2:8). At first glance, Paul's insistence on a rule of behavior seems at odds with his

---

[55] Paul Nadim Tarazi, "St. John Chrysostom: Exegesis for Preaching and Teaching," *Journal of the Orthodox Center for the Advancement of Biblical Studies, Vol 4, No 1,* 2011, ocabs.org/journal/index.php/jocabs/article/viewFile/40/15

warning "that a man is not justified by works" (2:16). A closer look at terminology exposes both Peter's and the implied reader's hypocrisy.

The word *dikaioō* (δικαιόω, from the same root as *dikaios;* δίκαιος) is rendered "justified" (2:17) in English, wrongly implying human merit where none is credited. A better translation—one reflecting the context of the letter—is the more literal "declared righteous," in which "justification" (2:21), *dikaiosúnē* (δικαιοσύνη, also from *dikaios*), is understood as a status bestowed in judgment (*dikaioō*) by one holding authority. [56] As with earlier examples (Abel, Sarah, and Jacob, etc.), no human being can claim to stand on his or her own merit. "The righteousness of a righteous man," explains Ezekiel, "will not deliver him in the day of his transgression" (Ezekiel 33:12). Since, according to Paul, "there is none righteous, not even one" (Romans 3:10), the purpose of the Law is to demonstrate Israel's inadequacy through imposed failure. Like the fictional *Kobayashi Maru*, [57] the Torah forms its disciples in wisdom by presenting a test that cannot be passed. Unlike its fictional analogue, the Lord's test cannot be cheated, since God's providence is incontrovertible. In Peter's own words, the Law was a yoke "which neither our fathers nor we have been able to bear" (Acts 15:10). There is no idea expressed, philosophy

---

[56] Paul Nadim Tarazi, *The Chrysostom Bible – Romans: A Commentary* (St. Paul, Minnesota: OCABS Press, 2010), 84.

[57] A fictional no-win scenario in *Star Trek* used to assess character when facing a life-threatening problem with no solution.

embraced, identity claimed, belief confessed, or action taken that makes the human being righteous before God. "The sacrifice acceptable to God," cries David, "is a broken spirit; a broken and humbled heart God will not despise" (Psalm 50:17). Through Christ, the Jew who is under the Law sees that he is no better than the gentile who is without the Law, since "God shows no partiality" (2:6; Deuteronomy 1:17 and 10:17). When we pass by a homeless man on the side of the road, we feel ashamed, because his public suffering is a reminder of our failure. Through Paul's teaching, the *shame* of the crucifixion fulfills the Law by *exposing* the Jew's uncleanness. In effect, the Jew was chosen by God to demonstrate that there is no difference between Israel and the nations! Does this make the gospel the *cause* or "agent" of the Jew's sin? Is the homeless man the *cause* of our greed? "Certainly not!" (2:17)

Powerless and without hope, those under the authority of the Law have only to accept their defeat "through the Law" (2:19) that their will might be "crucified with Christ" (2:20). This crucifixion gives way to the seed of God's will—not their own actions—as the source of life:

> When I say to the righteous he will surely live, and he so trusts
> in his righteousness that he commits iniquity, none of his
> righteous deeds will be remembered; but in that same iniquity
> of his which he has committed he will die. (Ezekiel 33:13)

Left with nothing but the hope of God's mercy, those under the Law now see the Law's purpose: to make known their indebtedness to God, that compelled by the same, they might show mercy to their neighbors. As each act of mercy is given in permanent debt to God, no one achieves anything of his or her own accord; all credit for our actions is deferred to God's will, which produces its work in us. In this way, it is not Paul who lives, but the content of the gospel that lives in him (2:20).

Sadly, it is Paul's opponents, not Paul, who exploit Christ as an "agent of sin" by using the Law to impose their Jewish identity (2:14). If, by placing their "trust" (πίστις) in Paul's teaching (2:16), the gentiles were found equally humbled, what more could Peter ask of them; of those who on account of wickedness, "turn" from their wickedness (Ezekiel 33:12)? What more could he demand of those whom God had already declared holy (Acts 10:15; 25–28)? By imposing circumcision, Peter had abandoned God's mercy, presuming himself above the weakness of Jesus; "building again," Paul writes, the earthly Jerusalem "destroyed" by God through the Prophets, as if "Christ died to no purpose" (2:21).

Chapter 3

The Resurrection

"You boast, 'We have made a covenant with death, and with Sheol we have made a pact. The overwhelming scourge will not reach us when it passes by, for we have made falsehood our refuge and we have concealed ourselves with deception.'" (Isaiah 28:15)

Nothing New Under the Sun

Galatians 3:1–5

3:1 O foolish Galatians! Who has bewitched you, before whose eyes Jesus Christ was publicly portrayed as crucified? 2 Let me ask you only this: Did you receive the Spirit by works of the Law, or by hearing with faith? 3 Are you so foolish? Having begun with the Spirit, are you now ending with the flesh? 4 Did you experience so many things in vain? — if it really is in vain. 5 Does he who supplies the Spirit to you and works miracles among you do so by works of the Law, or by hearing with faith?

3:1 Ὦ ἀνόητοι Γαλάται, τίς ὑμᾶς ἐβάσκανε τῇ ἀληθείᾳ μὴ πείθεσθαι, οἷς κατ᾽ ὀφθαλμοὺς Ἰησοῦς Χριστὸς προεγράφη ἐν ὑμῖν ἐσταυρωμένος; 2 τοῦτο μόνον θέλω μαθεῖν ἀφ᾽ ὑμῶν· ἐξ ἔργων νόμου τὸ Πνεῦμα ἐλάβετε ἢ ἐξ ἀκοῆς πίστεως; 3 οὕτως ἀνόητοί ἐστε; ἐναρξάμενοι πνεύματι νῦν σαρκὶ ἐπιτελεῖσθε; 4 τοσαῦτα ἐπάθετε εἰκῇ; εἴ γε καὶ εἰκῇ 5 ὁ οὖν ἐπιχορηγῶν ὑμῖν τὸ Πνεῦμα καὶ ἐνεργῶν δυνάμεις ἐν ὑμῖν, ἐξ ἔργων νόμου ἢ ἐξ ἀκοῆς πίστεως;

The Resurrection

It was the crucifixion, *not* the resurrection, that was "publically portrayed" before the Galatians' eyes (3:1). That God, who "supplies the Spirit and works miracles" (3:5), would demonstrate his power by hiding the resurrection is no more puzzling than Paul's insistence on the public display of Christ's embarrassing defeat. These two scriptural perplexities—the *public* cross and the *hidden* resurrection—prevent the depiction of human strength, stripping humanity of the power sought in its portrayal of the gods. The cross accomplishes this because anyone seeking power has nothing to boast of in a king who suffered defeat. The resurrection accomplishes this because the empty tomb *withholds* the depiction of God's victory from human eyes. Following the crucifixion, everyone who ran to the tomb in Mark was surprised and frightened to discover that the body of Jesus was *missing* (Mark 16:8). In all four gospels, *no one* was present to witness the resurrection taking place.

Before receiving Paul's teaching, the Galatians were fools to believe that the tomb of Jesus, a dead object "hewn out" by human hands "in the rock" (Matthew 27:60; Mark 15:46) was a living thing, able to provide life. In the New Testament, the empty tomb is akin to a rock face hollowed out by Roman stonecutters, with no statue to show for their efforts. "We know," Paul writes elsewhere, "that there is no such thing as an idol in the world, and that there is no God but one" (1 Corinthians 8:4). Just as this God had set his people free from slavery to Pharaoh, so too the gentiles had been rescued from the tyranny of

Rome. Like the Hebrew children in Egypt, they were set free for a specific purpose, to become the slaves of God:

Then the Lord said to Moses, 'Pharaoh's heart is stubborn; he refuses to let the people go. Go to Pharaoh in the morning as he is going out to the water, and station yourself to meet him on the bank of the Nile; and you shall take in your hand the staff that was turned into a serpent. You shall say to him, 'The Lord, the God of the Hebrews, sent me to you, saying, 'Let my people go, that they may serve me in the wilderness. But behold, you have not listened until now.'' (Exodus 7:14–16)

Having been liberated by God from the worship of Caesar, why would the Galatians now turn to another human master? "Having begun with the Spirit,"—the life-giving content of God's instruction—why were they "now ending with the flesh," placing their trust in the leaders of the church in Jerusalem? Like the people of Israel, the Galatians had repaid the Lord's generosity with cowardice and betrayal:

As Pharaoh drew near, the sons of Israel looked, and behold, the Egyptians were marching after them, and they became very frightened; so the sons of Israel cried out to the Lord. Then they said to Moses, 'Is it because there were no graves in Egypt that you have taken us away to die in the wilderness? Why have you dealt with us in this way, bringing us out of Egypt? Is this not the word that we spoke to you in Egypt, saying, 'Leave us alone that we may serve the Egyptians?' For it would have been better for us to serve the Egyptians than to die in the wilderness.'' (Exodus 14:10–12)

The Resurrection

Did God free the gentiles from one human oppressor only to enslave them to another? On the contrary, they were set free in order to follow God's life-giving instruction; yet, they *chose* death. "Vanity of vanities," cries the preacher, "all is vanity" (Ecclesiastes 1:2; 3:4)! O foolish Galatians:

> *"I am the Lord your God, who brought you out of the land of Egypt, out of the house of slavery. 'You shall have no other gods before me.'" (Exodus 20:2–3; Deuteronomy 5:6–7)*

Be Fruitful and Multiply

Galatians 3:6–9

6 Thus Abraham "believed God, and it was reckoned to him as righteousness." 7 So you see that it is men of faith who are the sons of Abraham. 8 And the scripture, foreseeing that God would justify the Gentiles by faith, preached the gospel beforehand to Abraham, saying, "In you shall all the nations be blessed." 9 So then, those who are men of faith are blessed with Abraham who had faith.

6 καθὼς Ἀβραὰμ ἐπίστευσε τῷ Θεῷ, καὶ ἐλογίσθη αὐτῷ εἰς δικαιοσύνην 7 Γινώσκετε ἄρα ὅτι οἱ ἐκ πίστεως, οὗτοί εἰσιν υἱοὶ Ἀβραάμ 8 προϊδοῦσα δὲ ἡ γραφὴ ὅτι ἐκ πίστεως δικαιοῖ τὰ ἔθνη ὁ Θεός, προευηγγελίσατο τῷ Ἀβραὰμ ὅτι ἐνευλογηθήσονται ἐν σοὶ πάντα τὰ ἔθνη 9 ὥστε οἱ ἐκ πίστεως εὐλογοῦνται σὺν τῷ πιστῷ Ἀβραάμ

According to Paul, no act of religious piety, however zealous, can raise up life from the dust of the earth. This teaching is forcefully expressed in Paul's understanding of the resurrection, in which God safeguards the continuation of life by raising Jesus, Abraham's offspring (3:16). Faced with Isaac's death, it was Abraham's trust in God, "who provides for himself" (Genesis 22:8), that saved his son, creating the possibility of abiding life for Isaac's children. "Those who trust in the Lord," cries David, "are like Mount Zion, which cannot be moved but abides forever" (Psalm 125:1). In the story of Isaac's sacrifice, the pressing issue is not the morality of murder, but Abraham's acceptance of God as sole progenitor and master (Genesis 21:1–2; 25:21).

The central theme of Genesis, echoed in Galatians, is God's struggle to ensure the continuation of life despite man's wayward progeny. [58] The chief instruction in Genesis, "be fruitful and multiply," is a call for each generation to submit to God's will so that the Lord can ensure life for its children. Underscoring this point, in Genesis, God intervenes to save the line of Abram, first by *preventing* Sarai's pregnancy:

> *So Sarai said to Abram, 'Now behold, the Lord has prevented me from bearing children. Please go in to my maid; perhaps I will obtain children through her.' (Genesis 16:2)*

In the example of Ishmael's conception, Sarai plotted with Abram to work around God to "obtain a child" from Hagar. As if to demonstrate the tyranny of human survival schemes, no sooner had Hagar conceived than Sarai

---

[58] Paul Nadim Tarazi, *The Chrysostom Bible – Genesis: A Commentary,* (St. Paul, Minnesota: OCABS Press, 2009), 73–75.

treated her harshly, causing her to flee (Genesis 16:6). Taken stubbornly from Abram's seed, in Paul's words, Ishmael "was born according to the flesh" (4:22), to a mother "in slavery with her children" (4:25), an allegory for the "present Jerusalem"—in Galatians—under the authority of James. As with Abraham's children from other slaves, Ishmael was to live "to the east" (Genesis 16:12) away from Isaac, Abraham's sole heir:

> *Now Abraham gave all that he had to Isaac; but to the sons of his concubines, Abraham gave gifts while he was still living, and sent them away from his son Isaac eastward, to the land of the east. (Genesis 25:5–6)*

Since it is "through Isaac" that the descendants of God's covenant are named (Genesis 21:12), at the time of his death all that Abraham had was bequeathed to Isaac. Here is Paul's exposition of the story:

> *For they are not all Israel who are descended from Israel; nor are they all children because they are Abraham's descendants, but: 'through Isaac your descendants will be named.' That is, it is not the children of the flesh who are children of God, but the children of the promise are regarded as descendants. (Romans 9:6–8)*

Succinctly, not all who "are Abraham's descendants" are the children of God. As a result of Sarah's disobedience, many of Abraham's descendants were consigned to slavery as children of Ishmael. It is this slavery that God is fighting to avert through the posterity of his will, which demanded Sarah's trust. Accordingly, it is not the scheming of Sarah (analogous to fleshly circumcision) that fulfills the commandment to "be fruitful," but *submission to God's will*. Procreation is indeed providential; so too was Sarah's inability to bear a child. Yet, both Sarah and the Pillars act as though they are able to provide children for Abraham! As if to foreshadow the consequences of Sarah's disobedience, Hagar, the mother of a people born into slavery, was an Egyptian.

Paul is explicit in his exegesis of the Torah. Sarah's pregnancy was possible only because Abraham trusted in the Lord's promise to provide children. "As good as dead," Abraham's body was beyond all hope of procreation (Hebrews 11:12; Romans 4:19):

Then the Lord took note of Sarah as he had said, and the Lord did for Sarah as he had promised. So Sarah conceived and bore a son to Abraham in his old age, at the appointed time of which God had spoken to him. (Genesis 21:1–2)

It was *the Lord* who made Sarah pregnant according to his promise. The text makes no mention of sexual relations between Abraham and Sarah. Likewise, in the New Testament, it is *the Lord* who takes action on behalf of David's posterity, fulfilling his promise to Abraham in the womb of Mary, who trusted in God's instruction:

And Mary said, 'Behold, the bondslave of the Lord; may it be done to me according to your word.' And the angel departed from her. (Luke 1:38)

The Resurrection

By a command, God made the heavens and the earth; by a promise, he gave a child to Sarah; by a word, he impregnated the womb of Mary, a virgin; likewise, by his will, he caused life to spring forth from a tomb of stone.

In the Bible, it is God's intervention through his Torah, not the work of the flesh, that ensures the continuation of life. According to Paul, only God has the power to bestow life upon the fallen, both Jew and gentile. "Follow me," Jesus said to Abraham's descendants, "and leave the dead to bury their dead" (Matthew 8:22).

Where the children of Adam repeatedly fail in Genesis, God succeeds as the righteous judge of his own deeds, echoed in the refrain: "And God saw that it was good" (Genesis 1). Matthew later applies this refrain to Jesus Christ, who, like Isaac, is not from a human seed (Matthew 3:17). Likewise, Luke joins the chorus: "Glory to God in the highest, and on earth peace among men," with whom God "is pleased" through the birth of Abraham's offspring, Jesus Christ (Luke 2:14).

Jacob, also Called Israel

Galatians 3:10–16

10 For all who rely on works of the Law are under a curse; for it is written, "Cursed be every one who does not abide by all things written in the book of the Law, and do them." 11 Now it is evident that no man is justified before God by the Law; for "He who through faith is righteous shall live"; 12 but the Law

*does not rest on faith, for "He who does them shall live by them."
13 Christ redeemed us from the curse of the Law, having
become a curse for us — for it is written, "Cursed be every one
who hangs on a tree" — 14 that in Christ Jesus the blessing of
Abraham might come upon the gentiles, that we might receive
the promise of the Spirit through faith. 15 Brothers and sisters,
I give an example from daily life: once a person's will has been
ratified, no one adds to it or annuls it. 16 Now the promises
were made to Abraham and to his offspring; it does not say,
"And to offsprings," as of many; but it says, "And to your
offspring," that is, to one person, who is Christ.*

10 Ὅσοι γὰρ ἐξ ἔργων νόμου εἰσίν, ὑπὸ κατάραν εἰσί·
γέγραπται γάρ· ἐπικατάρατος πᾶς ὃς οὐκ ἐμμένει ἐν πᾶσι τοῖς
γεγραμμένοις ἐν τῷ βιβλίῳ τοῦ νόμου τοῦ ποιῆσαι αὐτά· 11
ὅτι δὲ ἐν νόμῳ οὐδεὶς δικαιοῦται παρὰ τῷ Θεῷ, δῆλον· ὅτι ὁ
δίκαιος ἐκ πίστεως ζήσεται 12 ὁ δὲ νόμος οὐκ ἔστιν ἐκ
πίστεως, ἀλλ᾽ ὁ ποιήσας αὐτὰ ἄνθρωπος ζήσεται ἐν αὐτοῖς 13
Χριστὸς ἡμᾶς ἐξηγόρασεν ἐκ τῆς κατάρας τοῦ νόμου
γενόμενος ὑπὲρ ἡμῶν κατάρα· γέγραπται γάρ· ἐπικατάρατος
πᾶς ὁ κρεμάμενος ἐπὶ ξύλου· 14 ἵνα εἰς τὰ ἔθνη ἡ εὐλογία τοῦ
Ἀβραὰμ γένηται ἐν Χριστῷ Ἰησοῦ, ἵνα τὴν ἐπαγγελίαν τοῦ
Πνεύματος λάβωμεν διὰ τῆς πίστεως 15 Ἀδελφοί, κατὰ
ἄνθρωπον λέγω· ὅμως ἀνθρώπου κεκυρωμένην διαθήκην
οὐδεὶς ἀθετεῖ ἢ ἐπιδιατάσσεται 16 τῷ δὲ Ἀβραὰμ ἐρρήθησαν
αἱ ἐπαγγελίαι καὶ τῷ σπέρματι αὐτοῦ· οὐ λέγει, καὶ τοῖς
σπέρμασιν, ὡς ἐπὶ πολλῶν, ἀλλ᾽ ὡς ἐφ᾽ ἑνός, καὶ τῷ σπέρματί
σου, ὅς ἐστι Χριστός

In his commentary on Genesis, [59] Fr. Paul Tarazi
explains that among Abraham's children, it is Isaac who
was differentiated by faith. Where Jacob—also called

---

[59] Ibid.

Israel—wrestled with God (Genesis 32:24–32), placing conditions on his obedience (Genesis 28:20–21), Isaac exuded trust. Gifted with Rebekah's hand in marriage (Genesis 24:50–52) Isaac remained in the Promised Land during his courtship, embracing God's intervention through Abraham's arrangement of his marriage (Genesis 24:1–4). Later, Jacob plotted to obtain a wife of his own accord, ending up a slave in Laban's household, outside of Canaan,[60] like Ishmael, to "the east" (Genesis 29:1–18). Where Rachel, like Sarah, schemed jealously to obtain a child from Jacob's seed (Genesis 30:1–5), Isaac looked immediately to God for children (Genesis 25:20–21). Offered abundant life in God's household, as if to create life of his own accord, Jacob hedged his bets, pouring oil on a barren stone (Genesis 28:14–22). In the Ancient Near East, oil was considered a source of life, used to anoint the statues of the gods.[61] By every measure, Jacob, "the supplanter" (Genesis 25:26), was a lesser man than his father Isaac, who never wavered in trusting the Lord. The negative metaphor of Jacob's stone recurs in the account of his courtship, where he earns Rachel's favor by impressing her with his strength (Genesis 29:1–12).

In Mark, it is the Lord himself—not Jacob's children—who is able to remove the "large" stone covering the tomb of Jesus (Mark 16:1–4). In contrast, it was Jacob who in

---

[60] Ibid.,157–160.

[61] Jacob Milgrom, *Studies in Cultic Theology and Terminology* (Leiden, The Netherlands: E.J Brill, 1983), 153–154.

Genesis moved the "large" stone covering the mouth of the well (Genesis 29:2). In a show of strength, Jacob hoped to prove his own virility by securing life for Laban's flocks. Jacob's story is reframed by New Testament accounts of the resurrection. Running to the sepulcher with *arōmata* (ἀρώματα, fragrant oils) the women disciples missed the chance to anoint Jesus, since God—the sole progenitor—had already raised him (Mark 16:1; Luke 24:1). Significantly, the noun "Jacob" is the Hebrew antecedent of the Greek name "James." Taunting the Pillars, Matthew writes:

> *Do* not presume to say to yourselves, 'We have Abraham as our father'; for I tell you, God is able from these stones to raise up children to Abraham. (Matthew 3:9)

Faith and Works

Paul's admonition that no human being is justified by his or her own actions (3:11) brings the story of Isaac's trust to bear on the self-righteousness of Jacob's descendants. In a reversal of Jacob's mistreatment of Esau (Genesis 25:29–34; 27:34–36), in Galatians Jesus supplants Israel as the sole beneficiary of Abraham's bequest to Isaac (3:15; Genesis 25:5). As Tarazi explains, Isaac's trust in God's instruction to "sojourn" in Gerar without possessing the land, allotted peaceful coexistence with the Philistines, in fulfillment of God's promise. In effect, just as God's promise had produced Isaac, it took action on Isaac's behalf to ensure the continuation of his life.

In contrast with Jacob, who trusted in himself, striving "with God and man" (Genesis 32:28), an unassuming Isaac allowed God to protect him by offering no resistance to his enemies. Each time Abimelech's men commandeered one of his wells, a passive Isaac simply changed locations until his enemies left him in peace: "For now the Lord has made room for us, and we shall be fruitful in the land" (Genesis 26:22). It was the Lord who commanded fellowship with foreigners through circumcision; as such, it was the Lord's teaching that made Isaac fruitful, bringing peace with Abimelech. In sharing table fellowship with the Philistines (Genesis 26:30) Isaac foreshadowed the blessing that was to come upon the gentiles through the Eucharistic bread of Jesus Christ.

Like Isaac, when threatened by his enemies, Jesus acquiesced to God's instruction that human beings must submit to one another in love: "Father, if you are willing, remove this cup from me; yet not my will, but yours be done" (Luke 22:42). Worthy of the full litany of Deuteronomy's curses (3:10; Deuteronomy 27:15–26), Jerusalem and Rome had declared war on God by condemning an innocent man to death. Still, as one convicted and a faithful servant of his Father, innocent or not, Christ was subject to the requirements of the Law:

> *When someone is convicted of a crime punishable by death and is executed, and you hang him on a tree, his corpse must*

not remain all night upon the tree; you shall bury him that same day, for anyone hung on a tree is under God's curse. You must not defile the land that the Lord your God is giving you for possession. (Deuteronomy 21:22–23)

As directed by God, a passive and feeble Jesus allowed his enemies to hang him "on a tree," becoming "a curse" on our behalf—not by his actions—but through his submission to God's will. In Deuteronomy, hanging does not refer to the execution itself, but to the public shaming of the condemned following their execution.[62] This shame was put on public display as a warning to everyone of the fate that awaits those who do not keep the Law (Deuteronomy 21:21). For the Jew, who imagined it possible to keep the whole law, the shameful condemnation of the Messiah was a stumbling block; for the Roman, obsessed with honor and glory, it was a terrible embarrassment. It is no wonder, then, that the chief priests, along with the scribes and the elders, mocked Jesus, saying, "come down from the cross" (Matthew 27:41)!

By submitting to a shameful death, the penalty for Jacob's disobedience (3:13; Deuteronomy 21:20–21), Jesus redeemed Israel's children from slavery. The verb ἐξαγοράζω (3:13; to redeem, to rescue from ransom or

---

[62] Ronald Y. K. Fung, *The New International Commentary on the New Testament, Volume 9* (Grand Rapids, Michigan: Wm. B. Eerdman's Publishing Company, 1988), 147–148.

loss) commonly refers to the purchase of a slave's freedom.[63] Since even God cannot contradict his own law (3:15), having become a curse for us through the Law, Jesus fulfilled the Law's requirement on Jacob's behalf, securing life for Abraham's progeny:

> *So you shall keep his statutes and his commandments which I am giving you today, that it may go well with you and with your children after you, and that you may live long on the land which the Lord your God is giving you for all time. (Deuteronomy 4:40)*

The Return to Gerar

Galatians 3:17–29

> *17 This is what I mean: the Law, which came four hundred and thirty years afterward, does not annul a covenant previously ratified by God, so as to make the promise void. 18 For if the inheritance is by the Law, it is no longer by promise; but God gave it to Abraham by a promise. 19 Why then the Law? It was added because of transgressions, till the offspring should come to whom the promise had been made; and it was ordained by angels through an intermediary. 20 Now an intermediary implies more than one; but God is one. 21 Is the Law then against the promises of God? Certainly not; for if a law had been given which could make alive, then righteousness would indeed be by the Law. 22 But the scripture consigned all things to sin, that what was promised to faith in Jesus Christ might be*

---

[63] Paul Nadim Tarazi, *Galatians: A Commentary* (Crestwood, New York: St. Vladimir's Seminary Press, 1994), 129.

given to those who believe. 23 Now before faith came, we were confined under the Law, kept under restraint until faith should be revealed. 24 So that the Law was our custodian until Christ came, that we might be justified by faith. 25 But now that faith has come, we are no longer under a custodian; 26 for in Christ Jesus you are all sons of God, through faith. 27 For as many of you as were baptized into Christ have put on Christ. 28 There is neither Jew nor Greek, there is neither slave nor free, there is neither male nor female; for you are all one in Christ Jesus. 29 And if you are Christ's, then you are Abraham's offspring, heirs according to promise.

17 τοῦτο δὲ λέγω· διαθήκην προκεκυρωμένην ὑπὸ τοῦ Θεοῦ εἰς Χριστὸν ὁ μετὰ ἔτη τετρακόσια καὶ τριάκοντα γεγονὼς νόμος οὐκ ἀκυροῖ, εἰς τὸ καταργῆσαι τὴν ἐπαγγελίαν 18 εἰ γὰρ ἐκ νόμου ἡ κληρονομία, οὐκέτι ἐξ ἐπαγγελίας· τῷ δὲ Ἀβραὰμ δι᾽ ἐπαγγελίας κεχάρισται ὁ Θεός 19 Τί οὖν ὁ νόμος; τῶν παραβάσεων χάριν προσετέθη, ἄχρις οὗ ἔλθῃ τὸ σπέρμα ᾧ ἐπήγγελται, διαταγεὶς δι᾽ ἀγγέλων ἐν χειρὶ μεσίτου 20 ὁ δὲ μεσίτης ἑνὸς οὐκ ἔστιν, ὁ δὲ Θεὸς εἷς ἐστιν 21 Ὁ οὖν νόμος κατὰ τῶν ἐπαγγελιῶν τοῦ Θεοῦ; μὴ γένοιτο εἰ γὰρ ἐδόθη νόμος ὁ δυνάμενος ζῳοποιῆσαι, ὄντως ἂν ἐκ νόμου ἦν ἡ δικαιοσύνη· 22 ἀλλὰ συνέκλεισεν ἡ γραφὴ τὰ πάντα ὑπὸ ἁμαρτίαν, ἵνα ἡ ἐπαγγελία ἐκ πίστεως Ἰησοῦ Χριστοῦ δοθῇ τοῖς πιστεύουσι 23 Πρὸ δὲ τοῦ ἐλθεῖν τὴν πίστιν ὑπὸ νόμον ἐφρουρούμεθα συγκεκλεισμένοι εἰς τὴν μέλλουσαν πίστιν ἀποκαλυφθῆναι 24 ὥστε ὁ νόμος παιδαγωγὸς ἡμῶν γέγονεν εἰς Χριστόν, ἵνα ἐκ πίστεως δικαιωθῶμεν· 25 ἐλθούσης δὲ τῆς πίστεως οὐκέτι ὑπὸ παιδαγωγόν ἐσμεν 26 πάντες γὰρ υἱοὶ Θεοῦ ἐστε διὰ τῆς πίστεως ἐν Χριστῷ Ἰησοῦ· 27 ὅσοι γὰρ εἰς Χριστὸν ἐβαπτίσθητε, Χριστὸν ἐνεδύσασθε 28 οὐκ ἔνι Ἰουδαῖος οὐδὲ Ἕλλην, οὐκ ἔνι δοῦλος οὐδὲ ἐλεύθερος, οὐκ ἔνι ἄρσεν καὶ θῆλυ· πάντες γὰρ ὑμεῖς εἷς ἐστε ἐν Χριστῷ Ἰησοῦ 29 εἰ δὲ ὑμεῖς Χριστοῦ, ἄρα τοῦ Ἀβραὰμ σπέρμα ἐστὲ καὶ κατ᾽ ἐπαγγελίαν κληρονόμοι

What Isaac received as gift, Jacob refused, trusting himself in lieu of God's promise. As a result, subsequent generations lived in Egypt—outside of Canaan—for "four hundred and thirty years" (Exodus 12:40).

Having seen the affliction of his people in Egypt (Exodus 3:7), the Lord—through an angel—called upon Moses, an "intermediary" (3:19), to safeguard Jacob's descendants (3:23–24) until the realization of the promise to grant Abraham many children. Given specifically to mitigate Jacob's stubbornness, the Law of Moses, like the tree of knowledge in Genesis, was set in place as a stumbling block, so that in their stumbling the people would come to recognize their dependence on God as the only source of life (3:19–20). Since the Law and the promise both originate from God, the two cannot be in conflict (3:20–21). Likewise, under no circumstances can a ruling of God's divine court, "ordained by angels," annul a prior decision by God himself (3:17). *Stare decisis,*[64] the Law of Moses defers to the precedent set by God's promise to Abraham.

Through Jesus Christ, this promise, manifest in the Lord's provision for Isaac at Gerar, had now come to Israel (3:19, 25). Just as Isaac found life living side by side with the Philistines, so too could the "Jew" find life living in

---

[64] John Harrison Watts and Cliff Roberson, *Law and Society: An Introduction* (Boca Raton, Florida: CRC Press, 2014), 189. *Stare Decisis,* literally, "to stand by that which is decided." A previous decision by the highest court is binding on all other courts.

fellowship with the "Greek" (3:28). Enumerating this point, Paul extends the Lord's fellowship to include the disenfranchised of Roman society, placing women and slaves on a par with men and free citizens of the empire. Given to remove all social barriers, biblical circumcision had realized its fulfillment through baptism into Jesus Christ (3:27). To "put on Christ" is to be as Abraham was, "as good as dead," with no alternative but to place one's trust in the Lord (Romans 4:19; Hebrews 11:12). "Observe how the lilies of the field grow," taught Jesus, "They do not toil nor do they spin, yet I say to you that not even Solomon in all his glory clothed himself like one of these" (Matthew 6:28-29).

Chapter 4

Freedom in Christ

"The Spirit of the Lord God is upon me, because the Lord has anointed me to bring good news to the afflicted; He has sent me to bind up the brokenhearted, to proclaim liberty to captives and freedom to prisoners." (Isaiah 61:1)

There Is No "Them"

Galatians 4:1–7

4:1 I mean that the heir, as long as he is a child, is no better than a slave, though he is the owner of all the estate; 2 but he is under guardians and trustees until the date set by the father. 3 So with us; when we were children, we were slaves to the elemental spirits of the universe. 4 But when the time had fully come, God sent forth his Son, born of woman, born under the Law, 5 to redeem those who were under the Law, so that we might receive adoption as sons. 6 And because you are sons, God has sent the Spirit of his Son into our hearts, crying, "Abba! Father!" 7 So through God you are no longer a slave but a son, and if a son then an heir.

4:1 Λέγω δέ, ἐφ᾽ ὅσον χρόνον ὁ κληρονόμος νήπιός ἐστιν, οὐδὲν διαφέρει δούλου, κύριος πάντων ὤν, 2 ἀλλὰ ὑπὸ ἐπιτρόπους ἐστὶ καὶ οἰκονόμους ἄχρι τῆς προθεσμίας τοῦ πατρός 3 οὕτω καὶ ἡμεῖς, ὅτε ἦμεν νήπιοι, ὑπὸ τὰ στοιχεῖα τοῦ κόσμου ἦμεν δεδουλωμένοι· 4 ὅτε δὲ ἦλθε τὸ πλήρωμα τοῦ χρόνου, ἐξαπέστειλεν ὁ Θεὸς τὸν υἱὸν αὐτοῦ, γενόμενον ἐκ γυναικός, γενόμενον ὑπὸ νόμον, 5 ἵνα τοὺς ὑπὸ νόμον ἐξαγοράσῃ, ἵνα τὴν υἱοθεσίαν ἀπολάβωμεν 6 Ὅτι δέ ἐστε υἱοί, ἐξαπέστειλεν ὁ Θεὸς τὸ Πνεῦμα τοῦ υἱοῦ αὐτοῦ εἰς τὰς καρδίας ὑμῶν, κρᾶζον· ἀββᾶ ὁ πατήρ 7 ὥστε οὐκέτι εἶ δοῦλος, ἀλλ' υἱός· εἰ δὲ υἱός, καὶ κληρονόμος Θεοῦ διὰ Χριστοῦ

Himself a Pharisee and a Benjaminite (Philippians 3:4–6), Paul emphasizes the gospel's abolition of "Jew" and "Greek" (3:28) by personally identifying with the gentiles, who were considered "common or unclean" (Acts 10:25–28). While Jacob's descendants were "no better" than slaves, kept safe under the Law's guardianship (4:1–2), "we," Paul turns to the Greeks, "were slaves to the elemental spirits" (4:3), that is, to the pagan gods, "who by nature are not gods" (4:8). Sent by God at the appointed time (4:4), Jesus, also a slave, purchased the freedom of Jacob's descendants (4:5) so that "we," the gentiles, could serve the Lord "in the wilderness" (Exodus 7:16) with them, having been adopted as children of the one God (4:5). "Because you," the gentiles, are now God's children through Jesus, Paul continues, "we"—Jew and gentile together—are invited to call upon God as "Abba! Father!" (4:6) The juxtaposition of the Jewish-Aramaic "Abba" and the Greek "Pater" reinforces this unity, as Jew and gentile address God, the "Father" of all, with one voice:

> *"But I say to you, love your enemies, and pray for those who persecute you in order that you may be sons of your Father who is in heaven; for he causes his sun to rise on the evil and the good, and sends rain on the righteous and the unrighteous." (Matthew 5:44–45)*

Paul, Apostle and Scriptural Parent

Galatians 4:8–20

8 Formerly, when you did not know God, you were in bondage to beings who by nature are not gods; 9 but now that you have come to know God, or rather to be known by God, how can you turn back again to the weak and beggarly elemental spirits, whose slaves you want to be once more? 10 You observe days, and months, and seasons, and years! 11 I am afraid I have labored over you in vain. 12 Brethren, I beseech you, become as I am, for I also have become as you are. You did me no wrong; 13 you know it was because of a bodily ailment that I preached the gospel to you at first; 14 and though my condition was a trial to you, you did not scorn or despise me, but received me as an angel of God, as Christ Jesus. 15 What has become of the satisfaction you felt? For I bear you witness that, if possible, you would have plucked out your eyes and given them to me. 16 Have I then become your enemy by telling you the truth? 17 They make much of you, but for no good purpose; they want to shut you out, that you may make much of them. 18 For a good purpose it is always good to be made much of, and not only when I am present with you. 19 My little children, with whom I am again in travail until Christ be formed in you! 20 I could wish to be present with you now and to change my tone, for I am perplexed about you.

8 Ἀλλὰ τότε μὲν οὐκ εἰδότες Θεὸν ἐδουλεύσατε τοῖς μὴ φύσει οὖσι Θεοῖς· 9 νῦν δὲ γνόντες Θεόν, μᾶλλον δὲ γνωσθέντες ὑπὸ Θεοῦ, πῶς ἐπιστρέφετε πάλιν ἐπὶ τὰ ἀσθενῆ καὶ πτωχὰ στοιχεῖα, οἷς πάλιν ἄνωθεν δουλεύειν θέλετε; 10 ἡμέρας παρατηρεῖσθε καὶ μῆνας καὶ καιροὺς καὶ ἐνιαυτούς; 11 φοβοῦμαι ὑμᾶς μήπως εἰκῇ κεκοπίακα εἰς ὑμᾶς 12 Γίνεσθε ὡς ἐγώ, ὅτι κἀγὼ ὡς ὑμεῖς, ἀδελφοί, δέομαι ὑμῶν οὐδέν με

ἠδικήσατε 13 οἴδατε δὲ ὅτι δι᾽ ἀσθένειαν τῆς σαρκὸς
εὐηγγελισάμην ὑμῖν τὸ πρότερον, 14 καὶ τὸν πειρασμόν μου
τὸν ἐν τῇ σαρκί μου οὐκ ἐξουθενήσατε οὐδὲ ἐξεπτύσατε, ἀλλ᾽
ὡς ἄγγελον Θεοῦ ἐδέξασθέ με, ὡς Χριστὸν Ἰησοῦν 15 τίς οὖν
ἦν ὁ μακαρισμὸς ὑμῶν; μαρτυρῶ γὰρ ὑμῖν ὅτι εἰ δυνατὸν τοὺς
ὀφθαλμοὺς ὑμῶν ἐξορύξαντες ἂν ἐδώκατέ μοι 16 ὥστε
ἐχθρὸς ὑμῶν γέγονα ἀληθεύων ὑμῖν; 17 ζηλοῦσιν ὑμᾶς οὐ
καλῶς, ἀλλὰ ἐκκλεῖσαι ὑμᾶς θέλουσιν, ἵνα αὐτοὺς ζηλοῦτε 18
καλὸν δὲ τὸ ζηλοῦσθαι ἐν καλῷ πάντοτε καὶ μὴ μόνον ἐν τῷ
παρεῖναί με πρὸς ὑμᾶς 19 τεκνία μου, οὓς πάλιν ὠδίνω, ἄχρις
οὗ μορφωθῇ Χριστὸς ἐν ὑμῖν 20 ἤθελον δὲ παρεῖναι πρὸς
ὑμᾶς ἄρτι καὶ ἀλλάξαι τὴν φωνήν μου, ὅτι ἀποροῦμαι ἐν ὑμῖν

It was not the Galatians who sought God in wisdom, but God who chose them—through Paul's teaching—to become his children (4:9). Having identified with their weakness for this purpose, Paul is perplexed by their refusal to become children of Abraham like him (4:12). Instead, they turn to the Pillars, who "make much" of the gentiles (4:17), heaping praise to gain control. They "make much of you," he explains (ζηλοῦσιν ὑμᾶς, literally, "they court you"), because they want to keep you in need of them, flirting with you only to "shut you out" (4:17). In contrast, Paul assumes a fatherly role, speaking truth at the risk of alienation (4:16). It is "good," he explains, when children are "made much of" for the "good purpose" (4:18) of having the gospel of Jesus Christ "formed" in them (4:19).

In their first encounter with Paul, the Galatians fared much better. Paul's illness (4:13) was both an opportunity and a test of their submission to his teaching (4:14). Although he was a burden, they received Paul as an "angel" (God's messenger), as if he were Christ himself. Why then did the Galatians, once content with Paul's blessing, suddenly reject their father (4:15)? Why did they "turn back" (4:9) to the flesh, observing "days, and months, and seasons, and years" (4:10)?[65] Like Jacob, the Galatians had declined the Lord's gracious offer in favor of a business transaction: *if* we do these things, *then* we are righteous. As functionaries of the earthly temple, Paul's opponents were all too eager to please. "Perplexed" by his children, Paul was like a mother "in travail," struggling to give birth to progeny in the gospel (4:19).

Having failed the test of his absence, Paul expressed his wish to be present for the Galatians as a father, correcting their behavior. In the welcomed judgment of a parent's presence, the need for harsh words subsides (4:20).

The Jerusalem Above

Galatians 4:21–31

21 Tell me, you who desire to be under law, do you not hear the Law? 22 For it is written that Abraham had two sons, one by a slave and one by a free woman. 23 But the son of the slave was born according to the flesh, the son of the free woman through promise. 24 Now this is an allegory: these women are

---

[65] The marking of seasons is a reference to temple service (Genesis 1:14) but may also allude to the *ouoróros* (οὐροβόρος, literally, "tail-eating" snake) an ancient pagan symbol representing the never-ending cycle of life and death in the natural world.

two covenants. One is from Mount Sinai, bearing children for slavery; she is Hagar. 25 Now Hagar is Mount Sinai in Arabia; she corresponds to the present Jerusalem, for she is in slavery with her children. 26 But the Jerusalem above is free, and she is our mother. 27 For it is written, "Rejoice, O barren one who does not bear; break forth and shout, you who are not in travail; for the children of the desolate one are many more than the children of her that is married." 28 Now we, brethren, like Isaac, are children of promise. 29 But as at that time he who was born according to the flesh persecuted him who was born according to the Spirit, so it is now. 30 But what does the scripture say? "Cast out the slave and her son; for the son of the slave shall not inherit with the son of the free woman." 31 So, brethren, we are not children of the slave but of the free woman.

21 Λέγετέ μοι οἱ ὑπὸ νόμον θέλοντες εἶναι· τὸν νόμον οὐκ ἀκούετε; 22 γέγραπται γὰρ ὅτι Ἀβραὰμ δύο υἱοὺς ἔσχεν, ἕνα ἐκ τῆς παιδίσκης καὶ ἕνα ἐκ τῆς ἐλευθέρας 23 ἀλλ᾽ ὁ μὲν ἐκ τῆς παιδίσκης κατὰ σάρκα γεγέννηται, ὁ δὲ ἐκ τῆς ἐλευθέρας διὰ τῆς ἐπαγγελίας 24 ἅτινά ἐστιν ἀλληγορούμενα· αὗται γάρ εἰσι δύο διαθῆκαι, μία μὲν ἀπὸ ὄρους Σινᾶ, εἰς δουλείαν γεννῶσα, ἥτις ἐστὶν Ἅγαρ· 25 τὸ γὰρ Ἅγαρ Σινᾶ ὄρος ἐστὶν ἐν τῇ Ἀραβίᾳ, συστοιχεῖ δὲ τῇ νῦν Ἱερουσαλήμ, δουλεύει δὲ μετὰ τῶν τέκνων αὐτῆς· 26 ἡ δὲ ἄνω Ἱερουσαλὴμ ἐλευθέρα ἐστίν, ἥτις ἐστὶ μήτηρ πάντων ἡμῶν 27 γέγραπται γάρ· εὐφράνθητι στεῖρα ἡ οὐ τίκτουσα, ῥῆξον καὶ βόησον ἡ οὐκ ὠδίνουσα· ὅτι πολλὰ τὰ τέκνα τῆς ἐρήμου μᾶλλον ἢ τῆς ἐχούσης τὸν ἄνδρα 28 ἡμεῖς δέ, ἀδελφοί, κατὰ Ἰσαὰκ ἐπαγγελίας τέκνα ἐσμέν 29 ἀλλ᾽ ὥσπερ τότε ὁ κατὰ σάρκα γεννηθεὶς ἐδίωκε τὸν κατὰ πνεῦμα, οὕτω καὶ νῦν 30 ἀλλὰ τί λέγει ἡ γραφή; ἔκβαλε τὴν παιδίσκην καὶ τὸν υἱὸν αὐτῆς· οὐ μὴ γὰρ κληρονομήσει ὁ υἱὸς τῆς παιδίσκης μετὰ τοῦ υἱοῦ τῆς ἐλευθέρας 31 Ἄρα, ἀδελφοί, οὐκ ἐσμὲν παιδίσκης τέκνα, ἀλλὰ τῆς ἐλευθέρας

A majority of early rabbinic sources share the understanding that non-Jewish slaves were to embrace Judaism as a path to freedom.[66] While the absence of slaves among first century Jews was a source of religious pride, many Galatians who had been "baptized into Christ" (3:26) remained slaves in the Roman Empire, suggesting a deficiency in Paul's gospel.[67] In this context, the Pillars' insistence on circumcision would have been difficult for the Galatians to resist. Still, according to Paul, the correspondence of Jewish identity with worldly freedom betrayed yet another misreading of Genesis. Setting themselves above God, the circumcision party chose to emphasize their affiliation with the "free woman" (4:22) as the cause of Jewish freedom.[68] Again, Isaac's scriptural freedom stemmed not from his human mother, but from the seed of God's promise to Abraham (4:23). In Genesis, it is God's covenant that sustains man or abases him (4:24) irrespective of the "womb that bore" him, or "the breasts that nursed" him (Luke 11:27). In this sense, the barren womb of Sarah "rejoices" (4:27) because her fruit is born "not of blood, nor of the will of the flesh, nor of the will of man, but of God" (John 1:13). It is God's promise, Paul exhorts, not Sarah's womb, that sets the Galatians free as children of their true "mother," the "Jerusalem above" (4:26). As the children of God's heavenly city, they are set

---

[66] Jonathan Schorsch, *Jews and Blacks in the Early Modern World* (New York: Cambridge University Press, 2004), 75.

[67] Tarazi, *Galatians, a Commentary*, 240–241.

[68] Ibid.

free—not to live as they choose in the Roman Empire—but to live in observance of God's commandments. "Let my people go," says the Lord, "that they may serve me in the wilderness. But behold, you have not listened until now" (Exodus 7).

Chapter 5

The Bread of the Gospel

"He humbled you and let you be hungry, and fed you with manna which you did not know, nor did your fathers know, that he might make you understand that man does not live by bread alone, but man lives by every word that proceeds out of the mouth of the Lord." (Deuteronomy 8:3)

Salvation Is from the Lord

Galatians 5:1–6

5:1 For freedom Christ has set us free; stand fast therefore, and do not submit again to a yoke of slavery. 2 Now I, Paul, say to you that if you receive circumcision, Christ will be of no advantage to you. 3 I testify again to every man who receives circumcision that he is bound to keep the whole law. 4 You are severed from Christ, you who would be justified by the Law; you have fallen away from grace. 5 For through the Spirit, by faith, we wait for the hope of righteousness. 6 For in Christ Jesus neither circumcision nor uncircumcision is of any avail, but faith working through love.

5:1 Τῇ ἐλευθερίᾳ οὖν, ᾗ Χριστὸς ἡμᾶς ἠλευθέρωσε, στήκετε, καὶ μὴ πάλιν ζυγῷ δουλείας ἐνέχεσθε 2 Ἴδε ἐγὼ Παῦλος λέγω ὑμῖν ὅτι ἐὰν περιτέμνησθε, Χριστὸς ὑμᾶς οὐδὲν ὠφελήσει 3 μαρτύρομαι δὲ πάλιν παντὶ ἀνθρώπῳ περιτεμνομένῳ ὅτι ὀφειλέτης ἐστὶν ὅλον τὸν νόμον ποιῆσαι 4 κατηργήθητε ἀπὸ τοῦ Χριστοῦ οἵτινες ἐν νόμῳ δικαιοῦσθε, τῆς χάριτος ἐξεπέσατε · 5 ἡμεῖς γὰρ Πνεύματι ἐκ πίστεως ἐλπίδα δικαιοσύνης ἀπεκδεχόμεθα 6 ἐν γὰρ Χριστῷ Ἰησοῦ οὔτε

*περιτομή τι ἰσχύει οὔτε ἀκροβυστία, ἀλλὰ πίστις δι᾽ ἀγάπης
ἐνεργουμένη*

According to God's will, written in scripture, the Galatians had been set free for a single purpose: to love and to serve God and each other (5:13). Whatever springs from this purpose is the accomplishment of God, since the commandments of the Law "were God's work, and the writing was God's writing engraved on the tablets" (Exodus 32:16). It is for this specific purpose, Paul exclaimed, "that Christ has set us free" (5:1). Unlike a Roman slave released from bondage, the Galatians are not "free" to do whatever pleases them (5:17). If they choose circumcision—the work of their own hands—they choose empty achievement and vainglory over the love prescribed by the Torah (5:3–4). It is this love that is fulfilled by Jesus (5:6), whose Father willed that he should die in shame rather than lift a finger against his neighbor. In effect, circumcision had become the Galatians' sacred cow:

> Then the Lord spoke to Moses, 'Go down at once, for your people, whom you brought up from the land of Egypt, have corrupted themselves. They have quickly turned aside from the way which I commanded them. They have made for themselves a molten calf, and have worshiped it and have sacrificed to it and said, 'This is your god, O Israel, who brought you up from the land of Egypt! "The Lord said to Moses, 'I have seen this people, and behold, they are an obstinate people.' (Exodus 32:7–9)

Like the people of Israel, the Galatians had fashioned a god from their own material gain (Exodus 32:2), risking the same judgment that befell Jacob and his descendants:

I am the Lord your God, who brought you out of the land of Egypt, out of the house of slavery. You shall have no other gods before me. You shall not make for yourself an idol, or any likeness of what is in heaven above or on the earth beneath or in the water under the earth. You shall not worship them or serve them; for I, the Lord your God, am a jealous God, visiting the iniquity of the fathers on the children, on the third and the fourth generations of those who hate me, but showing lovingkindness to thousands, to those who love me and keep my commandments. (Exodus 20:1–6)

By rejecting the Spirit and seeking righteousness from the flesh (3:3) the Galatians had embraced "a yoke of slavery" (5:1), crying, again, like Israel: "It would have been better for us to serve the Egyptians than to die in the wilderness!" (Exodus 14:12)

Self-severed (5:4) and "shut out," (4:17) the Galatians had jeopardized the promise of life that came through Abraham's offspring, placing themselves and subsequent generations at risk (Exodus 20:5). In this sense, Paul's reference to the "hope of righteousness" (5:5) is as much a warning as an encouragement, since scriptural righteousness is a gift hoped for, to be given or withheld by God at the judgment. "Stand fast," Paul exclaimed (5:1), because the "wicked will not stand in the judgment, nor sinners in the assembly of the righteous" (Psalm 1:5). To avoid such judgment, the Galatians need only submit to Paul's gospel. Instead of fighting to save themselves, they need only stand by, without fear, knowing that God fights on their behalf, just as he fought for his people in the liberation from bondage in Egypt:

> *Do not fear! Stand by and see the salvation of the Lord which he will accomplish for you today; for the Egyptians whom you have seen today, you will never see them again forever. The Lord will fight for you while you keep silent. (Exodus 14:13–14)*

A Little Leaven

Galatians 5:7–15

7 You were running well; who hindered you from obeying the truth? 8 This persuasion is not from him who calls you. 9 A little leaven leavens the whole lump. 10 I have confidence in the Lord that you will take no other view than mine; and he who is troubling you will bear his judgment, whoever he is. 11 But if I, brethren, still preach circumcision, why am I still persecuted? In that case the stumbling block of the cross has been removed. 12 I wish those who unsettle you would mutilate themselves! 13 For you were called to freedom, brethren; only do not use your freedom as an opportunity for the flesh, but through love be servants of one another. 14 For the whole law is fulfilled in one word, "You shall love your neighbor as yourself." 15 But if you bite and devour one another take heed that you are not consumed by one another.

7 Ἐτρέχετε καλῶς· τίς ὑμᾶς ἐνέκοψε τῇ ἀληθείᾳ μὴ πείθεσθαι; 8 ἡ πεισμονὴ οὐκ ἐκ τοῦ καλοῦντος ὑμᾶς 9 μικρὰ ζύμη ὅλον τὸ φύραμα ζυμοῖ 10 ἐγὼ πέποιθα εἰς ὑμᾶς ἐν Κυρίῳ ὅτι οὐδὲν

ἄλλο φρονήσετε · ὁ δὲ ταράσσων ὑμᾶς βαστάσει τὸ κρῖμα,
ὅστις ἂν ᾖ 11 ἐγὼ δέ, ἀδελφοί, εἰ περιτομὴν ἔτι κηρύσσω, τί
ἔτι διώκομαι; ἄρα κατήργηται τὸ σκάνδαλον τοῦ σταυροῦ 12
ὄφελον καὶ ἀποκόψονται οἱ ἀναστατοῦντες ὑμᾶς 13 Ὑμεῖς γὰρ
ἐπ᾽ ἐλευθερίᾳ ἐκλήθητε, ἀδελφοί· μόνον μὴ τὴν ἐλευθερίαν εἰς
ἀφορμὴν τῇ σαρκί, ἀλλὰ διὰ τῆς ἀγάπης δουλεύετε ἀλλήλοις
14 ὁ γὰρ πᾶς νόμος ἐν ἑνὶ λόγῳ πληροῦται, ἐν τῷ, ἀγαπήσεις
τὸν πλησίον σου ὡς σεαυτόν 15 εἰ δὲ ἀλλήλους δάκνετε καὶ
κατεσθίετε, βλέπετε μὴ ὑπ᾽ ἀλλήλων ἀναλωθῆτε

By "running well" (5:7), the Galatians had begun their discipleship in observance of the Sabbath, resting from the vain striving of their "own ways" (Isaiah 58:13).[69] Just as scriptural freedom is not freedom for its own sake, the Sabbath—a day of rest prescribed by the Torah (Exodus 20:8–10)—is not assigned for relaxation or inactivity. On the contrary, the biblical Sabbath is given to substitute one type of "running" (5:7) for another. Linked to the provision of God's commandments, throughout scripture, the Sabbath is presented as the starting line in a race given to test the assembly's obedience:[70]

> *If because of the Sabbath, you turn your foot from doing your own pleasure on my holy day, and call the Sabbath a delight, the holy day of the Lord honorable, and honor it, desisting from your own ways, from seeking your own pleasure and speaking your own word, then you will take delight in the Lord, and I will make you ride on the heights of the earth;*

---

[69] See John 4:6–8;34. Jesus is "wearied" by the vain striving of his disciples, resting in order to accomplish the work of his Father.

[70] Tarazi, *The Chrysostom Bible – Genesis: A Commentary*, 51.

and I will feed you with the heritage of Jacob your father, for the mouth of the Lord has spoken. (Isaiah 58:13–14)

Paul's concern in chapter 2, that he himself "might be running, or had run, in vain" (2:2), expressed his fear, now realized, that the Pillars' insistence on their "own ways" would hinder the gentiles from this obedience (5:7). Turning to the Prophets, Paul kept faith, choosing to receive this hindrance as a blessing—a divine yeast or agitation assigned by God—to make the bread of the gospel rise, feeding both Jew and gentile. [71] Lest the Galatians take credit for this outcome, Paul reminded them that his confidence was not in them, but in the Lord (5:10). It was *the Lord* who allowed the Pillars to persecute Paul (5:11). Likewise, it was *the Lord* who allowed Paul's opponents to cause trouble in Galatia (5:10) that the "stumbling block of the cross" might remain firmly in place (5:11).

Paul's hope that his opponents "mutilate themselves" (5:12) extends the prophetic metaphor. If, in performing circumcision on themselves—the work of their own hands—they fail miserably, the Pillars might finally turn to God, the only physician able to bestow life. Through this failure, the fulfillment of the Torah's purpose becomes possible: "You shall love your neighbor as yourself" (5:14). Consume the bread of the gospel and live; alternatively, consume each other and die (5:15).

---

[71] Tarazi, *Galatians, a Commentary,* 280.

All You Need Is Love

Galatians 5:16–26

16 But I say, walk by the Spirit, and do not gratify the desires of the flesh. 17 For the desires of the flesh are against the Spirit, and the desires of the Spirit are against the flesh; for these are opposed to each other, to prevent you from doing what you would. 18 But if you are led by the Spirit you are not under the Law. 19 Now the works of the flesh are plain: fornication, impurity, licentiousness, 20 idolatry, sorcery, enmity, strife, jealousy, anger, selfishness, dissension, party spirit, 21 envy, drunkenness, carousing, and the like. I warn you, as I warned you before, that those who do such things shall not inherit the kingdom of God. 22 But the fruit of the Spirit is love, joy, peace, patience, kindness, goodness, faithfulness, 23 gentleness, self-control; against such there is no law. 24 And those who belong to Christ Jesus have crucified the flesh with its passions and desires. 25 If we live by the Spirit, let us also walk by the Spirit. 26 Let us have no self-conceit, no provoking of one another, no envy of one another.

16 Λέγω δέ, πνεύματι περιπατεῖτε καὶ ἐπιθυμίαν σαρκὸς οὐ μὴ τελέσητε 17 ἡ γὰρ σὰρξ ἐπιθυμεῖ κατὰ τοῦ πνεύματος, τὸ δὲ πνεῦμα κατὰ τῆς σαρκός· ταῦτα δὲ ἀντίκειται ἀλλήλοις, ἵνα μὴ ἃ ἂν θέλητε ταῦτα ποιῆτε 18 εἰ δὲ Πνεύματι ἄγεσθε, οὐκ ἐστὲ ὑπὸ νόμον 19 φανερὰ δέ ἐστι τὰ ἔργα τῆς σαρκός, ἅτινά ἐστι μοιχεία, πορνεία, ἀκαθαρσία, ἀσέλγεια, 20 εἰδωλολατρεία, φαρμακεία, ἔχθραι, ἔρεις, ζῆλοι, θυμοί, ἐριθείαι, διχοστασίαι, αἱρέσεις, 21 φθόνοι, φόνοι, μέθαι, κῶμοι καὶ τὰ ὅμοια τούτοις, ἃ προλέγω ὑμῖν καθὼς καὶ προεῖπον, ὅτι οἱ τὰ τοιαῦτα πράσσοντες βασιλείαν Θεοῦ οὐ κληρονομήσουσιν 22 ὁ δὲ καρπὸς τοῦ Πνεύματός ἐστιν ἀγάπη, χαρά, εἰρήνη, μακροθυμία, χρηστότης, ἀγαθωσύνη, πίστις, 23 πραότης, ἐγκράτεια· κατὰ τῶν τοιούτων οὐκ ἔστι νόμος 24 οἱ δὲ τοῦ Χριστοῦ τὴν σάρκα ἐσταύρωσαν σὺν τοῖς παθήμασι καὶ ταῖς ἐπιθυμίαις 25 Εἰ ζῶμεν πνεύματι, πνεύματι καὶ στοιχῶμεν 26 μὴ γινώμεθα κενόδοξοι, ἀλλήλους προκαλούμενοι, ἀλλήλοις φθονοῦντες

The concept of a struggle between good and evil— whether of conscience or between ideologies—is common to all cultures, and was often expressed in ancient literature as a conflict between twin gods.[72] As the good twin's doppelgänger, or alter ego, evil was understood as the flip side of the same coin. Insofar as this understanding presumes that humanity has a "good side," it is totally foreign to the biblical tradition:

> Then the Lord saw that the wickedness of man was great on the earth, and that every intent of the thoughts of his heart was only evil continually. The Lord was sorry that he had made man on the earth, and he was grieved in his heart. (Genesis 6:5–6)

If the intent and thought of the human heart is "evil continually, from his youth up" (Genesis 8:21), the only hope for the Galatians is submission to a will that is "not from man" (1:1). In this sense, the lists presented in 5:19–21 (the flesh) and 5:22–23 (the Spirit) are not in competition with each other, as though on equal footing. The first describes Israel and the nations, which of their own accord have no hope of the kingdom of God (5:21). The second, often and wrongly described as a list of

---

[72] Jane Garry and Hasan El-Shamy, *Archetypes and Motifs in Folklore and Literature* (New York: M.E. Sharpe, Inc., 2005) 459.

human virtues, presents the possibility of hope for human beings through the provision of God's fruit, should they submit to his statement, "You shall love your neighbor as yourself" (5:14). If led by this rule—which opposes the flesh (5:17)—the human being is no longer consigned to perpetual failure under the Law (5:18) since "what is impossible with men"—the hope of God's kingdom—"is possible with God" (Luke 18:27).

Those who submit to love as their single priority are free from the requirements of the Law (5:18). In other words, in *apparent* contradiction with Exodus, the Galatians *are* free to say and do whatever they please, so long as their behavior has the love of neighbor as its single outcome. "Against such," Paul writes, "there is no law" (5:23). Tarazi notes that the works (τὰ ἔργα) of the flesh are presented in the plural, while the fruit (καρπὸς) of the Spirit is singular. This, he explains, stresses that love—absent from the Hellenistic catalogues of virtues—is the single fruit of the gospel from which all other blessings proceed.[73] This is underscored by the specific works listed in Galatians (5:19–21), which emphasize behaviors that lead to division and strife. Where the promiscuity of the flesh divides communities, causing factions and conflict, in a very practical sense, love enables cooperation and the building up of human fellowship. Applying the wisdom of Leviticus and Deuteronomy, Jesus exclaimed:

---

[73] Tarazi, *Galatians, a Commentary,* 297.

The Bread of the Gospel

'You shall love the Lord your God with all your heart, and with all your soul, and with all your mind.' This is the great and foremost commandment. The second is like it, 'You shall love your neighbor as yourself.' On these two commandments depend the whole Law and the Prophets. (Matthew 22:36–40)

Chapter 6

Torah to the Gentiles

"Let not the wise boast of their wisdom, or the strong boast of their strength, or the rich boast of their riches, but let the one who boasts boast about this: that they have the understanding to know me, that I am the Lord, who exercises kindness, justice and righteousness on earth, for in these I delight, declares the Lord." (Jeremiah 9:23–24)

Galatians 6:1–6

1 Brethren, if a man is overtaken in any trespass, you who are spiritual should restore him in a spirit of gentleness. Look to yourself, lest you too be tempted. 2 Bear one another's burdens, and so fulfill the Law of Christ. 3 For if any one thinks he is something, when he is nothing, he deceives himself. 4 But let each one test his own work, and then his reason to boast will be in himself alone and not in his neighbor. 5 For each man will have to bear his own load. 6 Let him who is taught the word share all good things with him who teaches.

6:1 Ἀδελφοί, ἐὰν καὶ προληφθῇ ἄνθρωπος ἔν τινι παραπτώματι, ὑμεῖς οἱ πνευματικοὶ καταρτίζετε τὸν τοιοῦτον ἐν πνεύματι πραότητος σκοπῶν σεαυτόν, μὴ καὶ σὺ πειρασθῇς 2 ἀλλήλων τὰ βάρη βαστάζετε, καὶ οὕτως ἀναπληρώσατε τὸν νόμον τοῦ Χριστοῦ 3 εἰ γὰρ δοκεῖ τις εἶναί τι μηδὲν ὤν, ἑαυτὸν φρεναπατᾷ 4 τὸ δὲ ἔργον ἑαυτοῦ δοκιμαζέτω ἕκαστος, καὶ τότε εἰς ἑαυτὸν μόνον τὸ καύχημα ἕξει καὶ οὐκ εἰς τὸν ἕτερον· 5 ἕκαστος γὰρ τὸ ἴδιον φορτίον βαστάσει 6 Κοινωνείτω δὲ ὁ κατηχούμενος τὸν λόγον τῷ κατηχοῦντι ἐν πᾶσιν ἀγαθοῖς

As the "spiritual" (πνευματικοί) are directed by the gospel's rule—*love your neighbor as yourself*—they can never correct a weaker brother of their own accord, but must walk "by the Spirit" of love's provision, expressed here as gentleness (5:25; 6:1). Paul's warning that the spiritual must look to themselves is a stern reminder that the church is not to be governed by its leaders. On the contrary, it is the rule of the Spirit, the content of the gospel, that is to direct human actions. Since "all men are liars" (Psalm 116:11), this rule is given in opposition to the human being. Human words, wisdom, judgments, and most importantly, *will,* are to be supplanted by the written gospel, lest the leaders of the church also "be tempted" to idolatry. In the end, the spiritual have only to take care of their neighbor, in fulfillment of Jesus Christ, who carries the Torah to the gentiles (6:2).

It is not the spiritual who are alive, but the Law of Christ that lives in them and is at work on their behalf (2:20). Anyone, Paul explains, who imagines himself a god when he is passing away, "deceives himself" (6:3). This deception will be exposed in the coming judgment, when the living God will hold the dead accountable for their actions (6:4) and make each person face the consequences of his or her behavior (6:5). Lest the weaker brother imagine himself greater than those set above him, Paul reminds those who have been taught the word that they too are expected to manifest its fruit, and will be judged accordingly (6:6). "A disciple," Jesus said, "is not above his teacher" (Matthew 10:24).

The Destruction of Jerusalem

Galatians 6:7–10

7 Do not be deceived; God is not mocked, for whatever a man sows, that he will also reap. 8 For he who sows to his own flesh will from the flesh reap corruption; but he who sows to the Spirit will from the Spirit reap eternal life. 9 And let us not grow weary in well-doing, for in due season we shall reap, if we do not lose heart. 10 So then, as we have opportunity, let us do good to all men, and especially to those who are of the household of faith.

7 Μὴ πλανᾶσθε, Θεὸς οὐ μυκτηρίζεται· ὃ γὰρ ἐὰν σπείρῃ ἄνθρωπος, τοῦτο καὶ θερίσει· 8 ὅτι ὁ σπείρων εἰς τὴν σάρκα ἑαυτοῦ ἐκ τῆς σαρκὸς θερίσει φθοράν, ὁ δὲ σπείρων εἰς τὸ πνεῦμα ἐκ τοῦ πνεύματος θερίσει ζωὴν αἰώνιον 9 τὸ δὲ καλὸν ποιοῦντες μὴ ἐκκακῶμεν· καιρῷ γὰρ ἰδίῳ θερίσομεν μὴ ἐκλυόμενοι 10 Ἄρα οὖν ὡς καιρὸν ἔχομεν, ἐργαζώμεθα τὸ ἀγαθὸν πρὸς πάντας, μάλιστα δὲ πρὸς τοὺς οἰκείους τῆς πίστεως

Approaching the end of his epistle, Paul continues to remind the church in Galatia that *actions have consequences.* "Do not be deceived," he writes, "God is not mocked," each person will be judged by the consequence of his or her behavior (6:7). In the Prophets, Israel's enemies invade Jerusalem because the people's behavior—out of line with God's teaching—*invites violence.* The Lord who made the heavens and the earth also made the rules that govern them; rules that cannot be cheated. Just as love brings fellowship, the self-righteous and hypocritical behavior of Jerusalem brings violence and suffering:

> *'As I live!' declares the Lord God, 'I take no pleasure in the death of the wicked, but rather that the wicked turn from his way and live. Turn back, turn back from your evil ways! Why then will you die, O house of Israel?' (Ezekiel 33:11)*

Applying this teaching to the church in Galatia, Paul bears witness to the Lord's instruction through Jeremiah, which warns against trusting in "deceptive words" that present a temple of stone—the work of the flesh—as though it is spiritual:

> *The word that came to Jeremiah from the Lord, saying, 'Stand in the gate of the Lord's house and proclaim there this word and say, 'Hear the word of the Lord, all you of Judah, who enter by these gates to worship the Lord!' Thus says the Lord of hosts, the God of Israel, 'Amend your ways and your deeds, and I will let you dwell in this place. Do not trust in deceptive words, saying, 'This is the temple of the Lord, the temple of the Lord, the temple of the Lord.' For if you truly amend your ways and your deeds, if you truly practice justice between a man and his neighbor, if you do not oppress the alien, the orphan, or the widow, and do not shed innocent blood in this place, nor walk after other gods to your own ruin, then I will let you dwell in this place, in the land that I gave to your fathers forever and ever. Behold, you are trusting in deceptive words to no avail.' (Jeremiah 7:1–8)*

Crying aloud with Jeremiah, Paul exclaims, "Do not be deceived!" Should the Galatians choose to mock God by worshipping perishable things (φθοράν) they will surely perish with them (6:7–8); should they turn to scripture as their guide, they will find life. Placing all his trust in the scriptural alternative, Paul encourages his children to stay the course (6:9), mindful of their first duty to "the household of faith," which is inclusive of both Jew and gentile (6:10). Unlike the man-made temple, which according to Jeremiah is *not* the house of the Lord (Jeremiah 7:4), this new community, the temple of Jesus Christ, is to open its gates to "all men," showing hospitality to strangers and compassion for the weak (Jeremiah 7:6), replacing violence with fellowship.

Galatians 6:11–13

11 See with what large letters I am writing to you with my own hand. 12 It is those who want to make a good showing in the flesh that would compel you to be circumcised, and only in order that they may not be persecuted for the cross of Christ. 13 For even those who receive circumcision do not themselves keep the Law, but they desire to have you circumcised that they may glory in your flesh.

11 Ἴδετε πηλίκοις ὑμῖν γράμμασιν ἔγραψα τῇ ἐμῇ χειρί 12 ὅσοι θέλουσιν εὐπροσωπῆσαι ἐν σαρκί, οὗτοι ἀναγκάζουσιν ὑμᾶς περιτέμνεσθαι, μόνον ἵνα μὴ τῷ σταυρῷ τοῦ Χριστοῦ διώκωνται 13 οὐδὲ γὰρ οἱ περιτετμημένοι αὐτοὶ νόμον φυλάσσουσιν, ἀλλὰ θέλουσιν ὑμᾶς περιτέμνεσθαι, ἵνα ἐν τῇ ὑμετέρᾳ σαρκὶ καυχήσωνται

It is tempting to assume that Paul's use of "large letters" indicates an elevated voice or special emphasis (6:11). In reality, the modern practice of capitalization was unknown in the ancient world.[74] In late antiquity, letters were typically dictated to professional scribes, who wrote in small, deliberate script.[75] By indicating a change in style, Paul is emphasizing the importance of the entire epistle, taken from the hand of the scribe to be sealed personally with his "own hand" (6:11).

Reiterating the letter's main argument, Paul offers one last reminder that human achievement, status, and affiliation—manifest here in the practice of circumcision—are transitory and incompatible with the crucifixion of Jesus (6:12). Since nothing short of Christ's shameful death can fulfill the requirements of the Law, the Pillars' insistence on circumcision is utter hypocrisy (6:13). In contrast with Jerusalem's leaders, Jesus walked in submission to God's will, satisfying the requirements of Deuteronomy, which led to his shameful death. Christ's trust in the will of the Father, like that of Isaac, never faltered. This trust makes way for the Father's intervention on behalf of his son, whom he raised from the dead (1:1) realizing the promise of life for Abraham's offspring. "Do not think that I came to abolish the Law or the Prophets," said Jesus. "I did not come to abolish but to fulfill" (Matthew 5:17).

---

[74] R. Alan Cole, *The Letter of Paul to the Galatians* (Grand Rapids, Michigan: Wm. B. Eerdmans Publishing Company, 1989), 233.
[75] Tarazi, *Galatians, a Commentary,* 320.

Galatians 6:14–18

14 But far be it from me to glory except in the cross of our Lord Jesus Christ, by which the world has been crucified to me, and I to the world. 15 For neither circumcision counts for anything, nor uncircumcision, but a new creation. 16 Peace and mercy be upon all who walk by this rule, upon the Israel of God. 17 Henceforth let no man trouble me; for I bear on my body the marks of Jesus. 18 The grace of our Lord Jesus Christ be with your spirit, brethren. Amen.

14 ἐμοὶ δὲ μὴ γένοιτο καυχᾶσθαι εἰ μὴ ἐν τῷ σταυρῷ τοῦ Κυρίου ἡμῶν Ἰησοῦ Χριστοῦ, δι᾽ οὗ ἐμοὶ κόσμος ἐσταύρωται κἀγὼ τῷ κόσμῳ 15 ἐν γὰρ Χριστῷ Ἰησοῦ οὔτε περιτομή τι ἰσχύει οὔτε ἀκροβυστία, ἀλλὰ καινὴ κτίσις 16 καὶ ὅσοι τῷ κανόνι τούτῳ στοιχήσουσιν, εἰρήνη ἐπ᾽ αὐτοὺς καὶ ἔλεος, καὶ ἐπὶ τὸν Ἰσραὴλ τοῦ Θεοῦ 17 Τοῦ λοιποῦ κόπους μοι μηδεὶς παρεχέτω· ἐγὼ γὰρ τὰ στίγματα τοῦ Κυρίου Ἰησοῦ ἐν τῷ σώματί μου βαστάζω 18 Ἡ χάρις τοῦ Κυρίου ἡμῶν Ἰησοῦ Χριστοῦ μετὰ τοῦ πνεύματος ὑμῶν, ἀδελφοί· ἀμήν

Divorced from the cross of Jesus, if Paul's opponents have only kept part of the Law, how are they better off than those who are without the Law? What right have they to boast? In contrast with Jerusalem, Paul boasts only of the cross of Jesus Christ, by which the power of the "present evil age" (1:4) is destroyed. Since Paul ascribes all glory to Jesus Christ, he himself has no power and the world has no power over him (6:14). In fulfillment of the Prophets, a new community has been formed, inclusive of both Jew and Greek; as such, circumcision and uncircumcision are no longer relevant (6:15). Those who walk according the rule of Paul's gospel *are* the "Israel of

God." All peoples, even slaves and foreigners, are now welcome in Abraham's household! As the apostle to this community, Paul does not bear witness to the fleshly marks of circumcision, but to the spiritual marks of the biblical word, since "the Law of God is in his heart," guiding and directing his steps (6:17; Psalm 37:31). Through Paul's teaching, this law—the rule of the Spirit—is open to all peoples as a word that is written not on the foreskin of human flesh but upon the heart, the seat of human reason.

Submit or Perish

Even as his opponents used circumcision to hide the shame of the cross (6:12) Paul, like Jeremiah, bore the spiritual "marks" of the gospel publicly, facing relentless persecution for its sake (6:17; 1 Corinthians 4:11–13). Since this teaching heralds the destruction of Jerusalem, it is never welcomed, least of all by the religious community:

> *O Lord, you have deceived me and I was deceived; You have overcome me and prevailed. I have become a laughingstock all day long; Everyone mocks me. For each time I speak, I cry aloud; I proclaim, 'Violence and destruction!' Because for me the word of the Lord has resulted in reproach and derision all day long. (Jeremiah 20:7–8)*

Here, Jeremiah laments his commission, which demands that he proclaim "violence and destruction" to his own people. "Behold," the Lord warned David, "I will raise up evil against you from your own household" (2 Samuel

12:11). In preaching the destruction of the flesh and its idols, Paul, like Jeremiah, draws the mockery and derision of his opponents, who empty the cross of its purpose, all the while working to undermine his apostolic ministry. Like Jeremiah, Paul's ministry earned him nothing but "reproach and derision all day long." It is easy to discredit a person who brings unpopular news. Nevertheless, the church need only look to the marks on Paul's broken body, whipped and beaten like the prophets, to see the validity of his apostleship (6:17). Enough! The time for debate is past! "Henceforth, let no man trouble me," thunders a prophetic Paul, submit to the love of the cross or perish!

Having laid down the rule of the gospel with apostolic authority, Paul seals his letter with the word "grace," delaying the day of "peace" to allow time for both Jew and gentile to "amend their ways and their doings" (Jeremiah 7:3). Since Paul's gospel has already appeared twice in Jerusalem, the possibility of a third visit portends final judgment.[76] Indeed, Paul's addressees will not see Jesus again until they say, "Blessed is he who comes in the name of the Lord" (Matthew 23:39)! If they heed the call of Jeremiah and change their behavior, God will provide life for them, in the land that he gave to their fathers forever (Jeremiah 7:7). Alternately, if they choose the flesh, they are free to perish as slaves. In the interim, should any

---

[76] Paul Nadim Tarazi, *Volume 66: Revelation, Orthodox Audio Bible Commentary* (St. Paul, Minnesota: OCABS Press, 2004).

questions arise, they are to listen once more to Paul's epistle, which begins as it ends, under the "grace" of God's instruction (1:3).

Teaching How to Love

"People think that when they enter church, they enter into the presence of the clergy. They actually think that what they hear in church they hear from us. They do not lay to heart, they do not consider, that they are entering into the presence of God and that it is he who addresses them. For when the reader standing up says, 'Thus says the Lord,' and the deacon stands and imposes silence on all, he is not honoring the reader, but him who speaks to all in the reading. If they knew that it was God who through his prophet speaks these things, they would cast away their pride."—John Chrysostom (2 Thessalonians, Homily III)

The fact that the love of neighbor is scripture's single objective is usually met with skepticism. "If that's *all* religion is about, why should I go to church?" Alternatively, "Why should I be Orthodox (or Catholic, or Protestant)?" From the perspective of the Bible, such questions are evil in every way imaginable. First, because those asking them, especially religious converts, seek to justify their choice of a particular church when "no man living is declared righteous" (Psalm 143:2; translation mine). Second, because for those who have been baptized into the death of Jesus Christ, it is forbidden to speak this way. Instead of setting their eyes on the Jerusalem above, they look to the city below; instead of seeking the kingdom of God, they seek worldly advancement for their own religious affiliation. Once down this path, the best of human intentions are undermined by our innate hypocrisy, making the love portrayed in the crucifixion impossible. Paul's letter to the Galatians is painfully clear: the self-preservation, self-interest, or worldly advancement of one's own religious community is *incompatible* with the gospel. "Woe to you, scribes and Pharisees, hypocrites! For you traverse sea and land to make a single proselyte, and when he becomes a proselyte, you make him twice as much a child of hell as yourselves." (Matthew 23:15)

A more nuanced objection to love is raised by theologians and religious scholars, who argue that the Bible *must* mean more than what is actually written. For such people, the empirical truth—that the Bible is simple, repetitive, and ruthlessly paternalistic—is dull and embarrassing. These either 1) impose their own theological complexity on the Bible, making it more interesting or palatable to them, 2) disregard those portions of the Bible that make them uncomfortable, or 3) disassemble scripture into "historical" fragments, stripping the biblical narrative of its continuity and authority. In each example, scholars wrest control from the text, setting themselves above God. How can a preacher speak with clarity or authority, they complain, when the Bible is so complex? By repeating scripture's obvious meaning in its own condescending tones, biblical pedagogy insults their intelligence, embarrassing them in the same way that teenagers are embarrassed by their parents. According to scripture, how could it be otherwise? By their own admission, the instruction to love is obvious and simple, yet no one is *doing it*. More than warranted, the condescension and insult found in scripture are necessary for biblical preaching.

Love is not complex. It is not the privileged jurisdiction of scholars nor a belief system to be debated by theologians. Love requires no special intelligence or affiliation. Love cannot be earned. Love has no need of religious institutions or the functionaries that serve them. On the contrary, love is an action made possible by the gift of humility, offered to humanity through its failures. That such wisdom is offered does not mean that all who fail become wise. For this reason, the Bible takes every opportunity to lord its instruction over our failures, propagating *its* wisdom at our expense. The Bible *glories* in human weakness. Every human loss or defeat is the Bible's teachable moment; every disaster—especially human suffering and violence—is seized upon by scripture as an opportunity to shame us; to ensure that our failure is complete, short of death. That the Greek philosophers excluded love from the catalogues of virtues is not a coincidence. Virtue is strength, and strength cannot tolerate the crucifixion of Jesus Christ.

The Disciple Is Not Above the Teacher

Learning how to love is like learning how to swim. It requires endless practice in the real world—endless hours in the pool—dealing with the primary data. In the case of love, this data is the wisdom gained from the shame of the cross. Such shame cannot be taught as classroom theory, with disciples peering down comfortably at the gospel as it floats in their theological petri dish. The students themselves must be the object of the lesson, in which the teacher's role is to facilitate a confrontation with biblical shame. This confrontation is not possible in American churches, where the roles of teacher and student are obscured. Such obfuscation devalues the word of God by demeaning the *exceptional* duty of those assigned to teach it. The role of the teacher is to explain and apply the content of the Bible for his or her disciples. This content comes down from above and must be preached as such. A teacher *must* be knowledgeable in the gospel or step aside. If knowledgeable, they *must* teach openly and *with authority* (Matthew 7:29) making no apologies for something that does not belong to them.

In Exodus, the first of all commandments dealing with our treatment of each other is the admonition to honor father and mother (Exodus 20:12). Following the prohibitions against idolatry, this commandment is given priority because it is impossible to love God if you are unwilling to submit to those whom he has established *over* or *against* you. God does not say, "honor your parents *if* they are honorable." In fact, the greater the shortcomings of parents, teachers and enemies, the more power the commandment holds for instruction. *All sin* is used by God for instruction, but especially the sins of those whom we fear or despise. There can be no doubt that Jerusalem feared Paul the persecutor at least as much as they feared Roman tyranny. To the extent that a teacher's sins are useful for instruction, *grace abounds* (Romans 5:20–21). "A little leaven," writes Paul, "leavens the whole lump" (5:9).

David was a murderer; Paul, an accomplice to murder; Peter, a traitor; James, a nepotist; and Jacob, a scheming hypocrite. The sum of such examples is as many as the stories of the Bible. Irrespective of their flaws, all these were blessed by God and assigned to carry out his teaching. In 1 Corinthians 4, when Paul boasts of fleshly inferiority, he lords his spiritual superiority over his children as their father in the gospel. He does so in order to shame them for the sake of edification. When Paul instructs the Corinthians, "be imitators of me," he refers not to his behavior, but to *his trust* in God's instruction, akin to Abraham's faith. This instruction is contained *in Paul's letter,* presented to the church in Corinth *as scripture.* Not only is the letter given *in Paul's absence,* but as the word of a *paterfamilias,* whose unique position precludes imitation by his children, let alone his household pedagogues, who are not fathers.[77]

To demand that a teacher lead by example is at once idolatrous and self-righteous. Idolatrous, because, as was the case with Jerusalem, it elevates the teacher above the Father's written instruction; self-righteous, because it sets the student above both. A student has *no right* to judge his or her teacher, not even to call the teacher "good"

---

[77] Paul Nadim Tarazi, *The Chrysostom Bible – 1 Corinthians: A Commentary* (St. Paul, Minnesota: OCABS Press, 2011), 95–96.

(Matthew 19:17; Mark 10:18; Luke 18:19). In the same way, teachers have *no right* to filter the Bible's content based on their assessment of audience, acting with partiality where God shows none (Galatians 2:6). To do so rejects Paul's admonition to gentleness (6:1) since it advances the yolk of human wisdom under the guise of Jesus Christ. Such behavior is akin to imposing circumcision! "It is a very small thing," Paul writes, "that I may be examined by you, or any human court; in fact, I do not even examine myself" (1 Corinthians 4:1). This does not mean that Paul is acquitted. On the contrary, both Paul and his disciples are *assumed guilty* until acquitted by God in the judgment. "Do not pass judgment before the time," Paul warns, "but wait until the Lord comes" (1 Corinthians 4:5). In anticipation of that day, Paul is responsible to teach *only* what is written:

> So that in us you may learn not to exceed what is written, so that no one of you will become arrogant in behalf of one against the other. For who regards you as superior? What do you have that you did not receive? And if you did receive it, why do you boast as if you had not received it? (1 Corinthians 4:6b–7)

Since all authority is ascribed to what is written, no one sets himself above the other. All in God's household are the slaves of Jesus Christ, who says to one, "go" to another "come" and to his slaves, "do this" (Matthew 8:9). Each accepts the duties they are given with gratitude, embracing their neighbor's station with the same, since all things are ordained by God (Romans 11:36). The teacher, by teaching; the student by submitting to instruction; and the Jew, by embracing the Greek. Only when we submit to this wisdom does the love of neighbor, and therefore, God's promise of life, become possible.